RAIN, TEMPERATURE AND CLIMATE CHANGE IN INDIA

GAURAV KUMAR SHANDILYA

RAIN, TEMPERATURE AND CLIMATE CHANGE IN INDIA
BY
GAURAV KUMAR SHANDILYA

ISBN-13: 978-93-341-6186-1

YEAR OF PUBLICATION: 2024

Cover design by: THE AUTHOR

TO NATURE AND ALL ITS CREATIONS, AND TO EVERY HAND RAISED IN ITS CONSERVATION, THIS BOOK IS A TRIBUTE TO YOUR ENDURING BEAUTY AND RELENTLESS PROTECTORS.

CONTENTS

PREFACE

Climate change is one of the most pressing issues of our time, affecting not only the environment but also the fabric of human society. In India, a country marked by its geographic diversity and socioeconomic challenges, the impacts of climate change are particularly pronounced. From devastating floods and unrelenting droughts to rising sea levels and erratic weather patterns, the consequences of climate change are directly influencing lives, livelihoods, and fundamental human rights.

This book, Rain, Temperature, and Climate Change in India, is an adaptation of my dissertation and delves deeply into the interconnectedness of climate change and its implications for human rights in India. It draws upon secondary sources, extensive research, and international reports to present a comprehensive study on this critical subject. The book is organized into six chapters, each addressing a key aspect of the climate change discourse:

Chapter 1: Introduction provides a foundational overview of climate change, setting the stage for a deeper understanding of its relevance to India's unique challenges.

Chapter 2: Causes, Indicators, and Effects of Climate Change examines the factors driving climate change, its measurable indicators, and the cascading effects on India's ecosystems and communities.

Chapter 3: Recent Climatic Disasters highlights case studies of recent climate-related disasters in India, such as cyclones, floods, and heatwaves, emphasizing their human and environmental toll.

Chapter 4: Climate Change and Human Rights explores the profound impact of climate change on fundamental human rights, including access to water, food security, health, and shelter.

Chapter 5: India's Actions Against Climate Change reviews the policies, strategies, and grassroots efforts being undertaken to mitigate and adapt to the challenges posed by climate change.

Chapter 6: Conclusion and Suggestions synthesizes the findings and offers actionable recommendations for policymakers, communities, and individuals to combat climate change and protect human rights.

This book aims to provide readers with a thorough understanding of climate change's multifaceted impact on India while also inspiring collective action to address these challenges. It is dedicated to nature and all those who tirelessly work to protect it, reflecting the urgency of our shared responsibility to conserve the environment for future generations.

I extend my gratitude to the researchers, institutions, and organizations whose work has significantly contributed to this study. It is my hope that this book will serve as a resource for academics, policymakers, and anyone passionate about safeguarding the environment and ensuring the dignity of human rights in the face of climate adversity.

Gaurav Kumar Shandilya

CHAPTER-1 : INTRODUCTION

INTRODUCTION

Ordinarily by climate change we mean a change of the climate that alters the composition of the global atmosphere. Such a change is attributed to the direct or indirect activities of human being. Growing human civilization and rapid industrialization with their expanded activities affect the thin layer of the atmosphere that surrounds the earth. Such an effect changes the natural atmosphere and the human civilizations as well as the future generations are going to suffer due to such changes in the natural system that governs the atmosphere.

The greenhouse gases which contribute significantly for the warming of the globe also are responsible in interfering in the global climate. Thus the concentration of greenhouse gases namely the carbon dioxide, methane, nitrous oxide and certain other heat trapping gases contribute in a significant manner for the changes that occur in the atmospheric climate. Carbon dioxide is produced when fossil fuels are burned and with the rapid depletion of forest cover, the effect of Carbon dioxide is further intensified.

Methane and Nitrous oxide are generally used in agricultural practices and the release of such gases causes certain effects on the lands and the land use and also the most important, the chlorofluorocarbons (CFCs) and other gases which have the capacity to trap the heat also account for changes in the climate.

Climate Of India

India's Geography And Geology Are Climatically Pivotal: The Thar Desert In The Northwest And The Himalayas In The North Work In Tandem To Effect A Culturally And Economically Break-All Monsoonal Regime. As Earth's Highest And Most Massive Mountain Range, The Mount Everest System Bars The Influx Of Frigid Katabatic Winds From The Icy Tibetan Plateau And Northerly Central Asia. Most Of North India Is Thus Kept Warm Or Is Only Mildly Chilly Or Cold During Winter; The Same Thermal Dam Keeps Most Regions In India Hot In Summer. Though The Tropic Of Cancer—The Boundary Between The Tropics And Subtropics—Passes Through The Middle Of India, The Bulk Of The Country Can Be Regarded As Climatically Tropical. As In Much Of The Tropics, Monsoonal And Other Weather Patterns In India Can Be Wildly Unstable: Epochal Droughts, Floods, Cyclones,

And Other Natural Disasters Are Sporadic, But Have Displaced Or Ended Millions Of Human Lives. There Is Widespread Scientific Consensus That South Asia Is Likely To See Such Climatic Events, Along With Their Aleatory Unpredictability, To Change In Frequency And Are Likely To Increase In Severity. Ongoing And Future Vegetative Changes And Current Sea Level Rises And The Attendant Inundation Of India's Low-Lying Coastal Areas Are Other Impacts, Current Or Predicted, That Are Attributable To Global Warming.

Being such a huge country, India exhibits a wide diversity of temperatures; from the freezing cold winters in the Himalayas to the scorching heat of the Thar Desert. The above two regions play a very significant role in controlling the weather of India, making it warmer than to be expected with its latitude. The Himalayas participate in this warming by preventing the cold winds from blowing in, and the Thar desert attracts the summer monsoon winds, which are responsible for making the majority of the monsoon season of India. However, the majority of the regions can be considered climatically tropical.

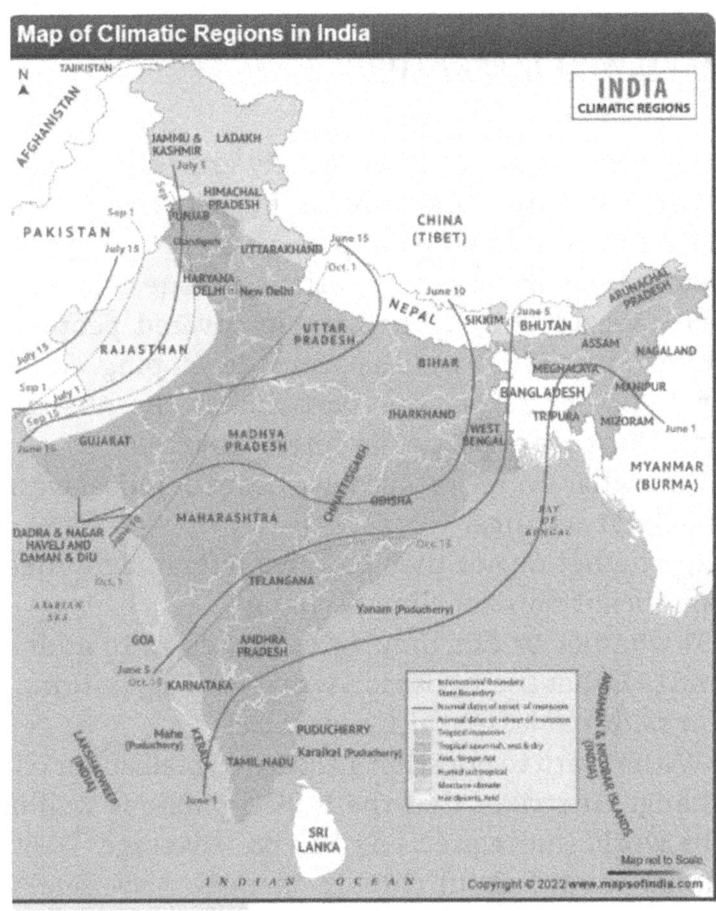

Source: www. mapsofIndia.com

REVIEW OF LITERATURE

In the summer of 2007, briefly after the publication of IPCC's Fourth Assessment Report, the BBC World Service commissioned a poll of 22,000 people in 21 countries with respect to various climate change issues (BBC World 2007). The sample covered people from industrialized as well as from developing countries. In India, 1,521 persons participated. Results to four questions are of particular interest here:
(1) To what degree people have heard of global warming or climate change,
(2) whether or not they perceive human activities as a significant cause of climate change,
(3) whether or not they agree on action to address it, and (4) what their position was regarding limiting GHG emissions in less-wealthy countries.

With regard to question 1 (heard or read about climate change) it strikes that the Indian public is well below the world (more precisely: the poll) average: 70% have heard or read about climate change on average, while only 48% in India. In contrast, the share of those who have not heard very much or nothing at all in India is 36% as opposed to 9% on average.

This result indicates that both the mass media coverage of climate change (or global warming) as well as its role in everyday communication in summer 2007 was relatively poor in India—at least the public impact of any possibly existing coverage. One might.

attribute this poor presence of climate change in India's public discourse to the relatively low stage of economic development—a very common argument both in developed and developing countries. While this assumption holds true in many cases (cf. Egypt, Kenya or Indonesia), people from countries with comparable levels of development have heard more of climate change (e.g. China, Philippines, Egypt, Brazil).

With respect to question 2 (humans as significant cause of climate change), much less Indians (47%) believe that climate change is caused by human activities than the sample average (79%), whereas slightly more Indians (21%) than on world average (14%) believe that human activity is not a significant cause. This low degree of attribution—in fact the lowest in the sample—gives rise to concern about (a) the public understanding of climate change science in India, as well as (b) to the prerequisites for mitigation action. On the other hand, one must not overlook the fact that more people in India agree that human activity is a significant cause of climate change than those believing the opposite.

When asked whether or not action is needed to address climate change, only a slight majority of Indian respondents agreed that major steps soon were needed (37% as compared to 65% on average), while 26% (average 25%) only wanted to see modest steps in the near future; 12% (average 6%) thought that it was not necessary to take any steps at all. Again, the comparison to China is interesting, as in this country 70% thought that major steps should soon be taken, and only 4% (even below world average) assumed no steps at all to be appropriate. Both countries find themselves in a structurally equal position: relatively 'early' stage of development, low per capita GHG emissions, up to now a low historical carbon footprint, large and growing total emissions, and a rejection of internationally binding emission reduction agreements, while at the same time taking some actions to improve energy efficiency and security. But only in China, a clear majority seems to support these policies by their personal attitudes.

A very interesting issue is raised by question 4: "Because total emissions from less wealthy countries are substantial and growing, these countries should limit their emissions of climate changing gases along with wealthy countries." Fifty-nine percent of the total sample hold this view, while 29% oppose it. In industrialized countries, consent is even more marked (USA: 75%, UK: 70%, Germany: 61%). The Indian respondents are clearly split: 33% agree that developing countries with substantial and growing emissions (such as India itself) should limit emissions, 29% oppose this view, and 43% are not decided. While respondents from the developing world tend to agree slightly less, India's rate of agreement ranks lowest in the total sample. Agreement in Nigeria is 42%, in Kenya 64%, and even in China, which finds itself addressed implicitly by the question, is 68%-the same as in Canada or the UK. If we compare the opposition to this point, i.e. people who think that less-wealthy countries should not be expected to limit their emissions, we find that the Indian value is lower than average. 53% of Egyptians, 50% of Nigerians, but also 49% of Italians or 34% in Germany hold that view.

We can conclude that the Indian public seems to be rather fragmented when it comes to limiting GHG emissions in India itself. The issue can receive no strong support, nor does it face strong opposition. A majority finds itself undecided. If combined with financial assistance and technology transfer, the situation changes, and almost half of the respondents would support emission caps for countries like India.

Jessica Barnes conducted a study on Contribution of anthropology to the study of climate change. Anthropology also contributes a broad, holistic outlook on society–environment relations, which draws attention to the fact that the new forms of production and consumption driving contemporary climate change are also altering people's livelihood strategies, modes of interaction and spatial and temporal horizons. Hence, climate change is accompanied everywhere by other kinds of change in society. Although climate is sometimes the dominant factor driving change, just as often it is outweighed by other factors. In some places people are talking and worrying about climate change, but in many places they are not. At larger spatial and temporal scales, the 'fingerprint' of anthropogenic climate change is easy to identify, and predictions of global temperature increase can be made with a fair level of certainty. But at the smaller scales at which everyday lives are affected and policy is implemented, it is far more difficult to attribute events and trends to climate change and project changes and their impacts. Climate change is becoming ever more prominent as an explanation for a wide range of social and economic issues, from crop failure to trans-border refugees, to issues of national and international security. In this context there is a danger that research and policy activities will marginalize other processes that are of more immediate significance to people's lives — such as grinding poverty or loss of arable land and biodiversity. Anthropologists can play a key role in helping to forestall what Hulme. identifies as 'climate reductionism' — a tendency to ascribe all changes in environment and society to climate. Anthropology illuminates the difficulty of unravelling climate change from the complex web of social and material relations that mediate people's interactions with their environments. Building on their interest in the capitalist systems that produce greenhouse gases, anthropologists can provide insights into the operation of such systems, which are making emissions reductions so politically and economically intractable today. Political institutions, personal relations and cultural meanings cannot be quantified or modelled in the same way as temperatures, but they strongly influence human action, need to be thoroughly understood and can be investigated with equal precision. The case of the Nile Basin illustrates this. Recent years have seen a significant increase in the funding from development agencies for climate change research and adaptation activities in the basin. International concern focuses on how a shift in precipitation patterns in the river's East African source regions under climate change could impact river discharge (at present general circulation models produce conflicting results as to the nature of that impact). Yet for farmers living in Egypt's Nile Valley and Delta, whose livelihoods depend on this water source, the amount of water they receive relates less to changes in precipitation thousands of kilometres away, and more to the engineering technologies and politics of water distribution decisions made in their immediate surroundings. Hence although climate change is a critical issue, focusing on climate change to the exclusion of, and in isolation from, other social, political, cultural and economic processes that shape landscapes and livelihoods is problematic.

Anthropological perspectives on climate change and sustainability: Implications for policy and action Hans A. Baer and Thomas Reuter, University of Melbourne

During the 1990s anthropologists Steve Rayner (Rayner and Malone 1998) and Mary Douglas (Douglas et al. 1998) as well as archaeologists Carol Crumley (1994) and Brian Fagan (2000) laid the foundations for the anthropology of climate change. Since then this field of anthropology has matured into a diverse and robust effort exemplified by four perspectives:

(1) the cultural ecological;

(2) the cultural interpretive;

(3) the critical anthropological perspective; and

(4) the applied anthropology perspective.

Many anthropologists are now asking questions from a cultural ecological perspective, examining all facets of human-environment relations. As part of the Arctic Climate Impact Assessment project, Mark Nuttall and his colleagues (Nuttall et al. 2004) examine the impact of climate change on subsistence patterns and adaptive strategies of indigenous Arctic peoples in the past and present. Ben Orlove (2005) examines climate variability in three frequently mentioned historical cases, namely the Mayan civilization of Mesoamerica, the Norse settlement of Greenland, and the U.S. Dust Bowl. Orlove (2005) and colleagues created the Initiative on Climate Adaptation Research and Understanding through the Social Sciences (ICARES). In her work on horse and cattle breeders in north-eastern Siberia, Susan Crate (2008) critiques what she regards as an excessive reliance on the concept of adaptation among policy makers as a way of avoiding serious mitigation efforts and global climate justice issues.

Most cultural interpretive or phenomenological examinations of climate change tend to focus on change perceptions on the part of diverse peoples, often through the lens of their "local knowledge". This perspective is the predominant one, given that it flows naturally from prior work that socio-cultural anthropologists have done on small-scale societies or local communities where they tend to gather data on people's "emic" (insider) views. While local knowledge may recognize the reality of climate change and other sustainability issues, for large segments of people, perhaps particularly the privileged, their specific cultural perceptions may also serve to downplay or even deny what is occurring, or that human activities have anything to do with it (Milton 1996). This creates a need to address culture specific change resistance (Reuter 2010).

The critical anthropology of climate change is guided by an eco-social perspective and by political ecology theory with its understanding of the politicized nature of human interaction with the environment (Baer and Singer 2009). It asks questions about the relationship of the capitalist mode of production to planetary sustainability, the role of power in the production and control (or non-control) of pollution, the unequal and unjust distribution of climate change effects, the contradictions of existing carbon mitigation and sustainability regimes and "green capitalism," and the many social movements that have emerged in opposition to corporate environmental degradation. It argues that global capitalism has come to embody so many contradictions that it must be transcended to ensure the survival of humanity on a sustained basis. This perspective calls for an alternative world system, committed to meeting people's basic needs, social equity and justice, democracy, environmental sustainability, and a safe climate.

In terms of applied work, anthropologists have been looking at sustainability issues at two broad and quite distinct levels, namely by participating in the formulation of environmental policies and by studying and becoming involved in the environmental movement which supports social, technological, and economic changes toward long-term sustainable practices. It is evident that more and more anthropologists will become involved as observers and engaged scholars in applied initiatives, seeking to respond to environmental change at the local, regional, national, and global level. This requires us to work as advisors in tangent with international climate regimes, national and state or provincial governments, NGOs and environmental groups, concerned communities, or climate action and sustainability movements.

Towards an integrated understanding

Anthropologists and other social scientists are not seeking to become climate scientists, agricultural scientists or ecologists. Conversely, natural scientists generally are not in a good position to develop a detailed understanding of the ways social systems operate, either at the macro- or the micro-levels, or how they contribute to climate change and various other forms of environmental damage. Efforts to examine and respond to the adverse impacts of human practice on nature and, conversely, of environmental degradation on humanity, has to be a multi-disciplinary one that entails collaboration between natural scientists and social scientists, including anthropologists, archaeologists, sociologists, political scientists, economists, and human geographers.

The reality is that natural scientists and economists continue to dominate much of the discourse on change, as is evidenced by the composition of the IPCC. Newer initiatives, such as Future Earth, established by ISSC and ICSU, already show a more balanced composition. Anthropologists and other social scientists are now playing a critical role in providing their analytical skills and insights to a larger struggle to create a world in which we learn to live in harmony with one another and the planet.

RATIONALE OF THE STUDY

The present study seeks to probe the steps taken at international and national level to save our earth from the disastrous effects of climate change, the adequacy of these steps and the steps that need to be taken in the short term and in the long term to save our planet 'earth'. When responding to the potential threat of climate change demands a complex response, addressing area as diverse as transportation, deforestation, power generation, control over natural resources, industrial and economic growth, and personal liberties, and hence the crossing of sectoral boundaries.

METHODOLOGY AND OBJECTIVES OF THE STUDY

Following objectives are formulated for the proposed study:

- To analyse the concept, indicator and causes and effect of climate change;
- To study about the linkage between human rights and climate change such as how human rights are affected by climate change and how specific group and section of society are more affected by climate change;
- To assess the role of indigenous people in climate change and how their knowledge can be used to adjust with climate change;
- To examine various policies and other measures by the government for the adaptation and mitigation of climate change in India.

DATA COLLECTION

This study was descriptive and was based on the secondary information but the primary data was collected through telephonic interview and social media chat with the people from various parts of India.

SECONDARY DATA SOURCES

- Research paper from SCOPUS, RESEARCH GATE, WEB OF SCIENCE, GOGLE SCHOLAR and J_STORE.
- Books related Climate Change and indigenous knowledge of tribal community.
- Libraries,
- Internet,
- Articles in various Newspapers & Magazines.

PRIMARY DATA SOURCES

- Telephonic interviews to the people able to talk on the subject of climate change.
- Social media chats

DELIMITATIONS OF THE STUDY

- ❖ The study was done by analyzing the secondary material basically, the actual sites ware not visited.
- ❖ The material on the study is quite vast and it is not possible to study all material.
- ❖ The time frame for the study is not sufficient for an extensive study

CHAPTER-2 : CAUSES, INDICATOR AND EFFECT OF CLIMATE CHANGE

CAUSES AND EFFECT OF CLIMATE CHANGE

All through the last three decades, the researcher opines that substantial attention has been given both to recognize the causes of the graving stresses on the environment and to evaluating their long term cost as well to the development of responsible strategies. Considering the increasing apprehension for the various environmental issues verified by the multiple gatherings organized by the scientific society, standard organizations and governments, the widespread space the environment is given in the media, and the concern articulated by the politician's one would tend to believe that the prediction of sufficient protective action to be taken would be promising. This seems however to be far from the case .The stresses on environment are getting more and more prominent. Relatively little has been done with regard to the global environmental harms which were recognized already in the 1960 and since then new major threats have surfaced. Clearly there are many causes causative to this reproachful development but there is a few which should be singled out as particularly important namely:

The speedy increase of the global population which is particularly dominated

in the developing world,

• The technological and socio-economic developments with their rising use of

chemicals in industry and agriculture resulting in expensive ecological

dilapidation.

• Lack of financial resources for environmental protection in less industrial and

the reckless attitude by the developed world.

• Deforestation.

• Burning of fossil fuels.

• Desertification.

Depletion of ozone layer.

• Global warming.

To comprehend climate change fully, the causes of climate change must have been divided into two categories:

Natural Causes

Volcanic eruption: when a volcano erupts it throws out huge volumes of sulphur dioxide, water vapor, dust and ash into atmosphere. Large volumes of gases and ash can influence climate patterns for years by escalating planetary reflectivity causing atmosphere cooling. Tiny particles called aerosol are formed by volcanoes.

Oceanic current: The oceans are a chief component of the climate system. Ocean currents move enormous amounts of the heat across the planet. Wind pushes parallel against the sea surface and drive oceans current patterns. Contacts between the ocean and atmosphere can also produce phenomena such as EL-Nino which occurs every 2-6 years. The oceans play an vital task in measuring the atmospheric absorption of CO2. Alteration in ocean circulation may influence the climate through the flow of CO2 into or out of the atmosphere.

Earth orbital changes: The earth makes one full path around the sun each year. It is leaning at an angle of 23.5 to the perpendicular plan of its orbital path. Changes in the tilt of the earth can lead to small but climatically crucial changes in the brawn of the seasons more tilt means warmer summers and colder winters.

Solar variations: The sun is the spring of energy from the earth's climate system. Although the suns energy output appears invariable from an everyday point of view, small changes over an extensive period of time can lead to climate changes. Some scientists suspect that a segment of the warming in the first half of the 20th century was due to increase in the output of solar energy. Scientific studies reveal that solar variations have performed a role in past climate changes. For instance a decline in solar activity was thought to have triggered the Little Ice Age between 1650 and 1850, when Greenland was largely cut off by ice from 1440 to 1720 and glaciers advanced in the Alps.

Human Causes

Industrial Revolution: Carbon discharge from industrial process and transport as well as agricultural emission like methane from livestock and manure, nitrous oxide from chemicals fertilizers.

Deforestation: Tropical forests are the richest forest resources of the world but tropical deforestation has become an environmental issue over the past five years. The annual deforestation in the tropics was anticipated to 11.4 million hectares in 1980 but now it has been estimated to be around 20.4 million hectares. Tropical deforestation has three causes which often act together in the same area. The first cause is permanent conversion of forest to agricultural land. Logging is another cause although deforestation depends on the methods and on what follows the logging. The third cause is the demand for fuel wood, fodder and other forest products where the resources cannot meet the demands

Droughts: Is an extended period of months or years when a region notes a deficiency in its water supply. Normally this occurs when a region receives constantly below average rainfall.

CHAPTER-3 : LINKAGE BETWEEN HUMAN RIGHTS AND CLIMATE CHANGE

Linkage Between Human Rights And Climate Change

The Human Rights Council has played a central role in drawing attention to the human rights dimensions of climate change. Importantly, in its resolution 10/4 (25 March 2009), the Council recognizes that—Climate change-related impacts have a range of implications, both direct and indirect, for the effective enjoyment of human rights. This was the first time the Council, or any other an inter-governmental body, unequivocally affirmed the negative human rights implications of climate change.

A OHCHR study on climate change and human rights (A/HRC/10/61) considered by the Human Rights Council in March 2009 gives examples of human rights affected by climate change-related effects and sets out some of the reasons why it is important and useful to apply a human rights framework to climate change

The Human Rights Council in its resolution 10/4 (25 March 2009) affirms that —human rights obligations and commitments have the potential to inform and strengthen international and national policy-making in the area of climate change.

International human rights norms and standards do not provide guidance as to specific technical and scientific aspects of climate mitigation and adaptation. Rather, human rights norms and standards set the parameters for how Government should act in response to climate change-related problems. More specifically, the integration of human rights in climate change-related action means giving due consideration to how human rights are affected by climate change impacts and by policies and measures to address climate change. It moves us beyond the aggregate cost benefit analysis which tend to dominate in I climate change debates, drawing attention to the need for a more disaggregated and sophisticated analysis to identify who will be affected by climate change and how, with a view to adjusting relevant policy measures accordingly. Equally, the human rights principles of equality, non-discrimination, transparency and accountability provide guidance for design and implementation of climate change

policies and measures.

Eight treaty bodies of the United Nations human rights treaty system have both monitoring and interpretive procedures:

i. the International Convention on Civil and Poletical Rights (ICCPR), whose treaty body is the human right committee,

ii. The International Covenant on Economic Social and Cultural Rights (ICESCR), which has the Committee on Economic, Social and Cultural Rights.

iii. The Convention against Torture (CAT), which has the Committee has the Committee Against Torture.

iv. The Convention on the Elimination of Racial Discrimination (CERD), which has the Committee on the Elimination of Racial Discrimination;

v. The Convention on the Elimination of Discrimination Against Women (CEDAW), which has the Committee on the Elimination of Discrimination Against Women;

vi. The Convention on the Rights of the Child (CRO, which has the Committee on the Rights of the Chi1d;

vii. The Convention on the Protection of the Rights of All Migrant Workers (CMW), which has the Committeeon Migrant Workers; and

viii. The Convention on the Rights of Persons with Dis abilities (CRPD), which has the Committeeon the Rights of Persons with Disabilities.

State Parties to each of these treaties are required to submit periodic reports detailing— the measures which they have adopted and progress made in achieving the observance of the rights recognized. The treaty bodies then examine the reports and communicate concerns and recommendations through Concluding Observations.

Current and Projected Impacts of Climate Change upon Humans

The human rights impacted by climate change have been recognized in many international human rights instruments, including the Universal Declaration of Human Rights (UDHR), the International Covenant on Civil anti Political Rights (ICCPR), the International Covenant on Economic, Social and Cultural Rights (ICESR), the. Convention on the Rights of the Child (CRC), the Convention on the Elimination of All Forms of Discrimination against Women (CEDAW), the Convention on the Elimination of Racial Discrimination (CERD), and selected Conventions adopted under the auspices of specialized agencies of the United Nations, in particular the ILO. Under these international treaties, the State has the primary duty not only to respect the covered rights, but to protect and fulfill these rights through positive action.

Current Impacts

i. There will be more deaths, disease, and injury due to the increasing frequency and intensity of heat waves, floods, storms, fires, and droughts.
ii. Rising sea levels will increase the risk of death and injury by drawing up to 20 per cent of the world's population

live in river basins that are likely to be affected by increased flood hazard by the 2080s.

iii. Heat waves are likely to increase deaths among elderly or chronically sick people, young children, and the socially is isolated Europe's 2003 heat wave–induced by climate change– resulted in 27,000 extra deaths.

iv. Future climate change is expected to put close to 50 million more people at risk of hunger by 2020, and an additional 132 million people by 2050.

v. In Africa, yields from rain-fed agriculture could fall by 50 per cent as soon as2020.

vi. In parts of Asia, food security will be threatened due to water shortages and rising temperatures. Crop yields could fall by up to 30 per cent in Central and South Asia by 2050.

vii. Water: By 2020, between 75 million and 250 million people in Africa are likely to face greater water stress due to climate change. Reduced water flow from mountain glaciers could affect up to one billion people in Asia by the 2050s

viii. Natural Resources : Approximately 20-30 per cent of plant and animal species assessed so far are likely to be at increased risk of extinction if average global temperatures rise more than 1.5—2.5°C. Coral bleaching and coastal erosion will affect fish stocks currently the primary source of animal protein for one billion people.

ix. Property and Shelter: Millions more people risk facing annual floods due to sea- level rise by the 2080s, mostly in the mega-deltas of Asia and Africa. On Small islands, too, sea-level rise is expected to exacerbate inundation, storm surge, and erosion, threatening vital infrastructure, settlements, and facilities that support the livelihoods of island communities.

x. Child malnutrition will increase, damaging growth and development prospects for millions of children.

xi. Increasing floods and droughts will lead to more cases of diarrhoea and cholera. Over 150,000 people are currently estimated to die each year from diarrhea, malaria, and malnutrition caused by climate change.

xii. Changing temperatures will cause some infectious diseases to spread into new areas. It is estimated that

220–400 million more people will be at risk of malaria. The risk of dengue fever is estimated to reach 3.5 billion people by 2085 due to climate change.

Impact on Population and Livelihood

Direct impact on the population and their livelihoods

- Rising sea-level and storms are direct causes of the flooding of territories, population displacement, salination of fresh-water resources, and diminishing habitable or cultivable land. These impacts in turn affect, for example, the right of self-determination, the right not to be deprived of one's means of subsistence, the right to own property, the right to life, the right to work, and the right to development.
- Rising surface temperatures also leads to greater occurrence of diseases such as scrub typhus, diarrheal diseases and other mosquito-borne diseases. These impacts affect, for example, the right to health and the right to life.
- The increasing number and intensity of weather events affects, for example, the rights to life, health, and housing.
- Receding coastlines and permafrost melting cause damage to land, houses, and other

infrastructure, affecting, for example, the right to an adequate standard of living, including the right to housing.

- Changes in precipitation patterns and the melting of glaciers affect access to water, an essential component of the right to water, as well as the ability to irrigate lands and Secure access to food, an essential component of the right to food.
- Mitigation actions relating to reducing emissions from deforestation and forest degradation (REDD) will affect. perhaps profo~ll1dly, the livelihoods, lifestyles, living conditions and cultures of indigenous peoples and other forest dwellers, affecting, for example, the right to enjoy culture and their way of life.

Human Rights And Climate Change

The Right To Life

The right to life is protected in both the UDHR and the [CCPR .Article 3 of the UDHR provides everyone has the right to life, liberty and security of person'. Article 6(1) of the ICCPR provides' every human being has the inherent right to life. This right shall be protected by law. No one shall be arbitrarily deprived of his life. The right to life of children also receives specific protection in article 6 of the CRC .In its General Comment on the right to life, the UN Human Rights Committee warned against interpreting the right to life in an arrow or restrictive manner. It stated that protection of this right requires the State to take positive measures and that 'it would be desirable for state parties to take all possible measures to reduce infant mortality and to increase life expectancy.

The quality of the environment affects the ability of people to enjoy the universally held right to life. Direct impacts include the increased incidents of natural disasters, while indirect impacts include poorest and of health, nutrition access to clean drinking water and more pro veto diseases.

The Right To Adequate Food

The right to adequate food is recognized in several international instruments; most comprehensively in the ICESCR. Pursuant to article 11(1), State parties recognize the right to everyone to an adequate standard of living for himself and his family, including adequate food, clothing and housing, and to the continuous improvement of living conditions, 'while pursuant to article 11(2) they recognize that more immediate and urgent steps may be needed to ensure the fundamental right to freedom from hunger and malnutrition.

The Right to Water

As the earth gets warmer, heat waves and water shortage will make it difficult to access safe drinking water and sanitation. There will be lower and more erratic rainfall in the tropical and sub-tropical areas of the Asia and the Pacific.

The 2007 OHCHR Report addressed the scope and content of human rights obligations related to safe drinking water and sanitation. Under ICCPR and ICESCR, the right to water provides for —equal and non-discriminatory access to a sufficient amount ofsafedrinkingwater for personal and domesticissues... to sustain life andhealth. The right to water is also specifically articulated is the article 24 of the CRC and article 14(2) (h) of the Convention on the Elimination of Discrimination against Women (CEDAW). In 2002 the UN Committee on Economic, Social and Cultural Rights recognized that water itself was an independent right. Drawing on a range of international treaties and declarations it stated, the right to water clearly falls within the category of guarantees essential for securing an adequate standard of living, particularly since it is one of the most fundamental conditions for survival.

The Right to Health

Health includes various necessary factors to dead a healthy like food, nutrition, housing access to safe water and a healthy environment. Climate change is likely to increase deaths from malnutrition, stress and infectious diseases worldwide.

A 2003 joint study by the World Health Organization and the London School of Hygiene and Tropical Medicine states that global warming may already be responsible for more than 160,000 deaths a year from malaria and malnutrition; a number that could double by 2020. Climate change will have many impacts on human health. It will affect the intensity of a wide range of diseases – vector-borne, water-borne and respiratory. In the pacific, changes in temperature and rainfall will make it harder to control dengue fever. Warmer climate will provide a more hospital environment for disease carrying mosquitoes. Article 25 of the UDHR states that everyone has the right to a standard adequate for the health and well-being of himself and his family. Article 12(a) of the ICESCR recognises the right of everyone to the enjoyment of the highest standard of physical and mental health. 'The right to health is also referred to in a number of articles in the CRC.

CHAPTER-4 : RECENT CLIMATIC DISASTERS

RECENT CLIMATIC DISASTERS IN INDIA

FLOOD

A flood is an overflow of water that submerges land which is usually dry. The European Union (EU) Floods Directive defines a flood as a covering by water of land not normally covered by water. In the sense of "flowing water", the word may also be applied to the inflow of the tide. Flooding may occur as an overflow of water from water bodies, such as a river or lake, in which the water overtops or breaks levees, resulting in some of that water escaping its usual boundaries, or it may occur due to an accumulation of rainwater on saturated ground in an areal flood. While the size of a lake or other body of water will vary with seasonal changes in precipitation and snow melt, these changes in size are unlikely to be considered significant unless they flood property or drown domestic animals.

Floods can also occur in rivers when the flow rate exceeds the capacity of the river channel, particularly at bends or meanders in the waterway. Floods often cause damage to homes and businesses if they are in the natural flood plains of rivers. While riverine flood damage can be eliminated by moving away from rivers and other bodies of water, people have traditionally lived and worked by rivers because the land is usually flat and fertile and because rivers provide easy travel and access to commerce and industry.

Some floods develop slowly, while others such as flash floods, can develop in just a few minutes and without visible signs of rain. Additionally, floods can be local, impacting a neighborhood or community, or very large, affecting entire river basins.

FLOODS IN INDIA

India is the most flood distressed state in the world after Bangladesh, accounting for 1/ 5th of the global deaths every year with 30 million people displaced from their homes yearly. Approximately 40 million hectares of the land is vulnerable to floods, with 8 million hectares affected by it. Unprecedented floods take place every year at one place or the other, with the most vulnerable states of India being Uttar Pradesh, Bihar, Assam, West Bengal, Gujarat, Orissa, Andhra Pradesh, Madhya Pradesh, Maharashtra, Punjab and Jammu & Kashmir.

The climatic history of India is studded with a very large number of floods, which have wreaked havoc on the country's economy.

1.FLOODS IN BIHAR

Bihar is India's most flood-prone State, with 76% of the population in the north Bihar living under the recurring threat of flood devastation. According to some historical data, 16.5% of the total flood affected area in India is located in Bihar while 22.1% of the flood affected population in India lives in Bihar. About 68,800 square kilometres (26,600 sq mi) out of total geographical area of 94,160 square kilometres (36,360 sq mi) comprising 73.06% is flood affected. Floods in Bihar are a recurring disaster which on an annual basis destroys thousands of human lives apart from livestock and assets worth millions. The 2013 Flood in Bihar affected more than 5.9 million people in 3,768 villages in 20 districts of the state.

A)1987 BIHAR FLOOD

The 1987 Bihar flood, caused by dramatic annual flooding of the Koshi River (nicknamed "the sorrow of Bihar"), was one of the worst floods in Bihar, India, in a decade. 1399 people and 5302 animals lost their lives and nearly 29 million people were affected in 30 districts, 382 blocks, 6,112 panchayat, and 24,518 villages. Government figures list damage to crops at an estimated 68 billion Indian rupees and damage to public property at 68 million rupees.

B) 2004 BIHAR FLOOD

The 2004 Bihar flood was one of the worst floods in Bihar, India in a decade. 885 people and 3272 animals had lost their lives and nearly 21.299 million human were affected. 20 districts of Bihar were affected. An alarming rise in water level due to heavy rains inundated fresh areas in Bhagalpur district, Begusarai district, Katihar district, Darbhanga district, Samastipur district and Khagaria district. According to the Central Water Commission Bagmati, BudhiGandak, KamlaBalan, Adhwara, Kosi and Mahananda rivers were flowing above the red mark at various places, while the Ganges crossed the danger mark for the first time at Farakka Barrage.

C) 2007 BIHAR FLOOD

The 2007 Bihar flood, which started in August 2007, was described by the United Nations as the worst flood in the "living memory" of Bihar. It is believed to be the worst flood in Bihar in the last 30 years. By 3 August, the estimated death toll was 41 people, and 48 schoolgirls were marooned in a school in the Darbhanga district. By 8 August, the flooding had affected an estimated 10 million people in Bihar. Army helicopters delivered food packets to Bihar residents and 180 relief camps were established. By 10 August, aid workers in Bihar reported that there was a dramatic increase of people with diarrhoea and by 11 August, flood deaths were still occurring.

D)2008 BIHAR FLOOD

It was one of the most disastrous floods in the history of Bihar, an impoverished and densely populated state in India. A breach in the Kosi embankment near the Indo-Nepal border (at Kusaha VDC, Sunsari district, Nepal) occurred on 18 August 2008. The river changed course and inundated areas which hadn't experienced floods in many decades. The flood affected over 2.3 million people in the northern part of Bihar.

E) 2013 BIHAR FLOOD

The 2013 Bihar Flood started in the month of July. The Flood caused a huge loss in the terms of life and property. According to State Government estimate 201 people lost their lives. Over 20 districts have been affected by the Flood. It is the most disastrous flood in the state after 2008 Bihar flood. More than 5.9 million people in 3,768 villages in 20 districts have been affected, officials say.

OTHER MAJOR FLOODS IN INDIA

2005: MAHARASHTRA FLOOD

The **2005 Maharashtra floods** refers to the flooding

of many parts of the Indian state of Maharashtra including large areas of the metropolis Mumbai a city located on the coast of the Arabian Sea, on the western coast of India, in which at least 5,000 people died. It occurred just one month after the June 2005 Gujarat floods. The term *26 July*, now is, in context always used for the day when the city of Mumbai came to a standstill.

Large numbers of people were stranded on the road, lost their homes, and many walked for long distances back home from work that evening. The floods were caused by the eighth heaviest ever recorded 24-hour rainfall figure of 994 mm (39.1 inches) which lashed the metropolis on 26 July 2005, and intermittently continued for the next day. 644 mm (25.4 inches) was received within the 12-hour period between 8am and 8pm. Torrential rainfall continued for the next week. The highest 24-hour period in India was 1,168 mm (46.0 inches) in Aminidivi in the Union Territory of Lakshadweep on 6 May 2004 although some reports suggest that it was a new Indian record. The previous record high rainfall in a 24-hour period for Mumbai was 575 mm (22.6 inches) in 1974.

Other places to be severely affected were Raigad, Chiplun, Khed, Ratnagiri and Kalyan in Maharashtra and the southern state of Goa.

The rains slackened between 28 July and 30 July but picked up in intensity on 31 July. The Maharashtra state government declared 27 July and 28 July as a state holiday for the affected regions. The government also ordered all schools in the affected areas to close on 1 August and 2 August. Mumbai Police commissioner Anami Narayan Roy requested all residents to stay indoors as far as possible on 31 July after heavy rains disrupted the city once again, grounding all flights for the day.

2005: GUJARAT FLOODS

The **2005 Gujarat Flood** was a bout of major flooding affecting many parts of Gujarat and was caused by heavy monsoon rains in June 2005.

Many of the southern districts of Gujarat were on flood alert. Rivers in the Valsad district were well above the flood level. About 15,000 people were evacuated from the coastal regions.

On June 30, the state was put on high alert and the army was asked to stand by for rescue and relief operations.

On July 1, the trains on the Ahmedabad-Mumbai line of Western Railway (India) were cancelled as the tracks near Vadodara were submerged. Helicopters of Indian Air Force were pressed into service to rescue some of the passengers stuck in the trains. With the exception of Ahmedabad airport most of the airports in the state were not operational. The Government of India announced relief package of Rs. 500 crores.

Due to these floods, crops worth crores of Rupees have been destroyed.

As of July 2 the death toll was about 123 people state

wide and more than 250,000 evacuated.

As of July 8, the rail traffic on the Ahmedabad-Mumbai railway lines was restored. The trains were running normally but with a restricted speed to ensure safety.

As of July 11, the loss due to flooding was estimated to be over Rs. 8000 crore (over 1.7 bn dollars).

2007 SOUTH ASIAN FLOODS

In 2007, global warming finally triggered a flood formation that was so devastating, that it annihilated the entire South Asian region, destroying large zones in India, Pakistan, Nepal, Bhutan and Bangladesh. It's most devastating effects were observed in South India, where it lasted for more than 15 days, killing more than 2000 people and affecting another 30 million. It was termed by UNICEF to be the worst flooding of South India in living memory.

2009 INDIAN FLOODS

The 2009 India floods affected various states of India in July 2009. The most affected states were Karnataka, Orissa, Kerala, Gujarat and North-East Indian states, with over 200 people reported dead, and a million homes destroyed.

2010 LADAKH FLOODS

On 6th August 2010, Leh and many other villages of

the Ladakh range were drowned by a downpour that killed at least 255 people, and resulted in a state loss of Rs.133crore. The unexpected heavy rainfall was attributed to the climatic changes resulting from global warming.

2011 INDIAN FLOODS

The 2011 surge of severe precipitation affected India savagely, with surging flood waters in Northern and Eastern India affecting more than 10 million people as the swollen rivers washed away roads and towns, particularly in the states of West Bengal, Bihar, Kerala and Assam.

2012 NORTHERN INDIAN FLOODS

The year 2012 is also included in the continuous chain of years of floods in India. In Assam, at least 27 people died and 900,000 were forced to evacuate their homes as monsoon rains drowned large areas. Starting on 4 Aug, unremitting showers fell on the northern states of Uttarakhand, Himachal Pradesh and Jammu, resulting in landslides, cloud bursts and flash floods. At least 34 people were killed and hundreds were made homeless.

2012 BRAHMAPUTRA FLOODS

The **2012 Brahmaputra floods** are an unprecedented flood event along the Brahmaputra river and its tributaries due to significant monsoon rains in India,

Bangladesh and Myanmar. 124 people have been killed by the flooding and landslides, and about six million people have been displaced. The worst hit area has been Assam state in India. Flooding has also significantly affected Kaziranga National Park, 540 animals have died including 13 rhinos.

In September 2011, the Brahmaputra River flowed through braided channels, but a year later, the channels could not be detected in the swollen river. During the monsoon season (June–October), floods are a common occurrence in India. Occasionally, massive flooding causes huge losses to crops, life and property. Deforestation in the Brahmaputra watershed has resulted in increased siltation levels, flash floods, and soil erosion in critical downstream habitat, such as the Kaziranga National Park in middle Assam.

Helicopters were deployed to drop food supplies to nearly 10,000 people in six villages where highway access was cut off by the flooding, about 550km west of Gauhati, the capital of Assam.

2012 HIMALAYAN FLASH FLOODS

2012 Himalayan flash floods are the floods that occurred on the midnight of August 3, 2012 in the Himalayan region of Northern Indian states. Many were dead and missing. Many places were affected. Landslides and flash floods were triggered by a sudden cloudburst which left 31 people dead while 40 are reported to be missing.

2013 ASSAM FLOODS

2013 Assam floods were floods in the Indian state of Assam which were triggered by heavy rainfall at the end of June in neighboring Arunachal Pradesh state through Brahmaputra river and its tributaries. These flood submerged 12 districts out of 27 in the state where more than 100,000 people affected. The flood also affected Kaziranga National Park and Pobitora Wildlife Sanctuary where many animals have moved on to higher ground to save themselves from the flood. The floods also affected some of the northern districts of Bangladesh where 100,000 people are suffering from a scarcity of food and pure drinking water.

2014 KASHMIR FLOODS

In September 2014, the Kashmir region suffered disastrous floods across many of its districts caused by torrential rainfall. The Indian administrated Jammu and Kashmir, as well as Pakistan administered Azad Kashmir, Gilgit-Baltistan and Punjab were affected by these floods. By September 24, 2014, nearly 277 people in India and 280 people in Pakistan had died due to the floods.

According to the Home Ministry of India, several thousand villages across the state had been hit and 390 villages had been completely submerged. In actual figures 2600 villages were reported to be affected in Jammu and Kashmir, out of which 390 villages in Kashmir were completely submerged. 1225 villages were partially affected and 1000 villages were affected in Jammu Division Many parts of Srinagar, including the Border Security Force (BSF) HQ in Sanant Nagar & Army cantonment in BadamBagh, were inundated, and vital roads were submerged, by the floods.

OTHER CLIMATIC DIASTERS IN INDIA

DROUGHTS

Drought in India has resulted in tens of millions of deaths over the course of the 18th, 19th, and 20th centuries. Indian agriculture is heavily dependent on the climate of India: a favorable southwest summer monsoon is critical in securing water for irrigating Indian crops. In some parts of India, the failure of the monsoons result in water shortages, resulting in below-average crop yields. This is particularly true of major drought-prone regions such as southern and eastern Maharashtra, northern Karnataka, Andhra Pradesh, Odisha, Gujarat, and Rajasthan.

History

In the past, droughts have periodically led to major Indian famines, including the Bengal famine of 1770, in which up to one third of the population in affected areas died; the 1876–1877 famine, in which over five million people died; and the 1899 famine, in which over 4.5 million died.

Impact of El Niño

All such episodes of severe drought correlate with El Niño-Southern Oscillation (ENSO) events. El Niño-related droughts have also been implicated in periodic declines in Indian agricultural output. Nevertheless, ENSO events that have coincided with abnormally high sea surfaces temperatures in the Indian Ocean—in one instance during 1997 and 1998 by up to 3 °C (5 °F)—have resulted in increased oceanic evaporation, resulting in unusually wet weather across India. Such anomalies have occurred during a sustained warm spell that began in the 1990s. A contrasting phenomenon is that, instead of the usual high pressure air mass over the southern Indian Ocean, an ENSO-related oceanic low pressure convergence center forms; it then continually pulls dry air from Central Asia, desiccating India during what should have been the humid summer monsoon season. This reversed air flow causes India's droughts. The extent that an ENSO event raises sea surface temperatures in the central Pacific Ocean influences the degree of drought. Around 43 per cent of

El Niño events are followed by drought in India.

CYCLONES

Intertropical Convergence Zone, may affect thousands of Indians living in the coastal regions. Tropical cyclogenesis is particularly common in the northern reaches of the Indian Ocean in and around the Bay of Bengal. Cyclones bring with them heavy rains, storm surges, and winds that often cut affected areas off from relief and supplies. In the North Indian Ocean Basin, the cyclone season runs from April to December, with peak activity between May and November. Each year, an average of eight storms with sustained wind speeds greater than 63 kilometres per hour (39 mph) form; of these, two strengthen into true tropical cyclones, which have sustained gusts greater than 117 kilometres per hour (73 mph). On average, a major (Category 3 or higher) cyclone develops every other year.

During summer, the Bay of Bengal is subject to intense heating, giving rise to humid and unstable air masses that produce cyclones. Many powerful cyclones, including the 1737 Calcutta cyclone, the 1991 Bangladesh cyclone and the 1999 Odisha cyclone have led to widespread devastation along parts of the eastern coast of India and neighboring Bangladesh. Widespread death and property destruction are reported every year in exposed coastal states such as Andhra Pradesh, Orissa, Tamil Nadu, and West Bengal. India's western coast, bordering the more placid Arabian Sea, experiences cyclones only rarely; these mainly strike Gujarat and, less frequently, Kerala.

In terms of damage and loss of life, Cyclone 05B, a supercyclone that struck Orissa on 29 October 1999, was the worst in more than a quarter-century. With peak winds of 160 miles per hour (257 km/h), it was the equivalent of a Category 5 hurricane. Almost two million people were left homeless; another 20 million people lives were disrupted by the cyclone. Officially, 9,803 people died from the storm; unofficial estimates place the death toll at over 10,100.

Disaster map of india-

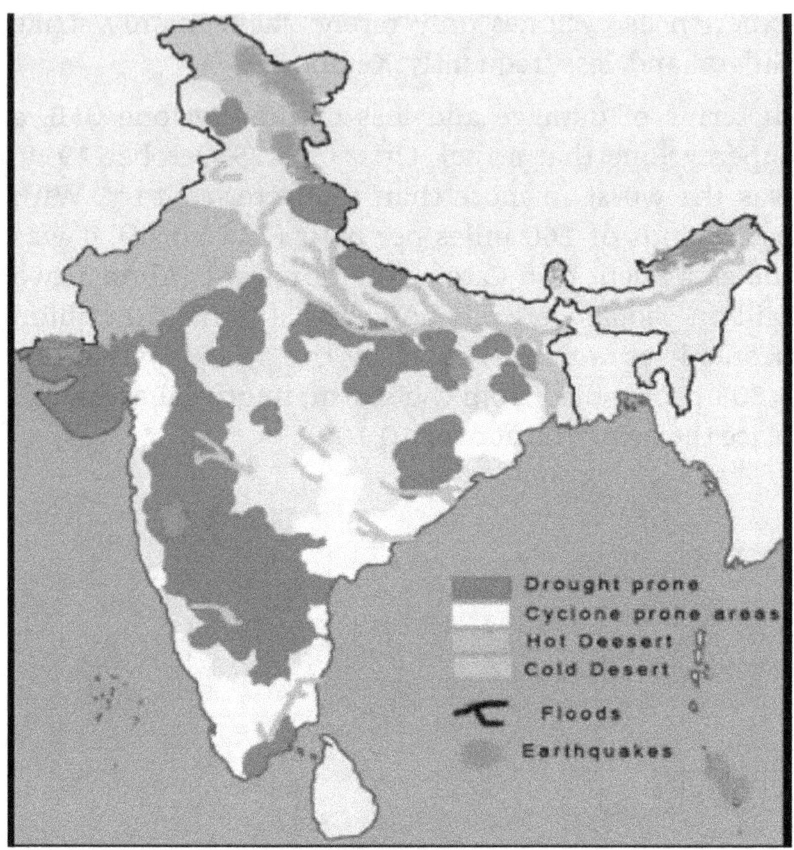

Source : www.mapsof India.com

Cyclone prone area in India

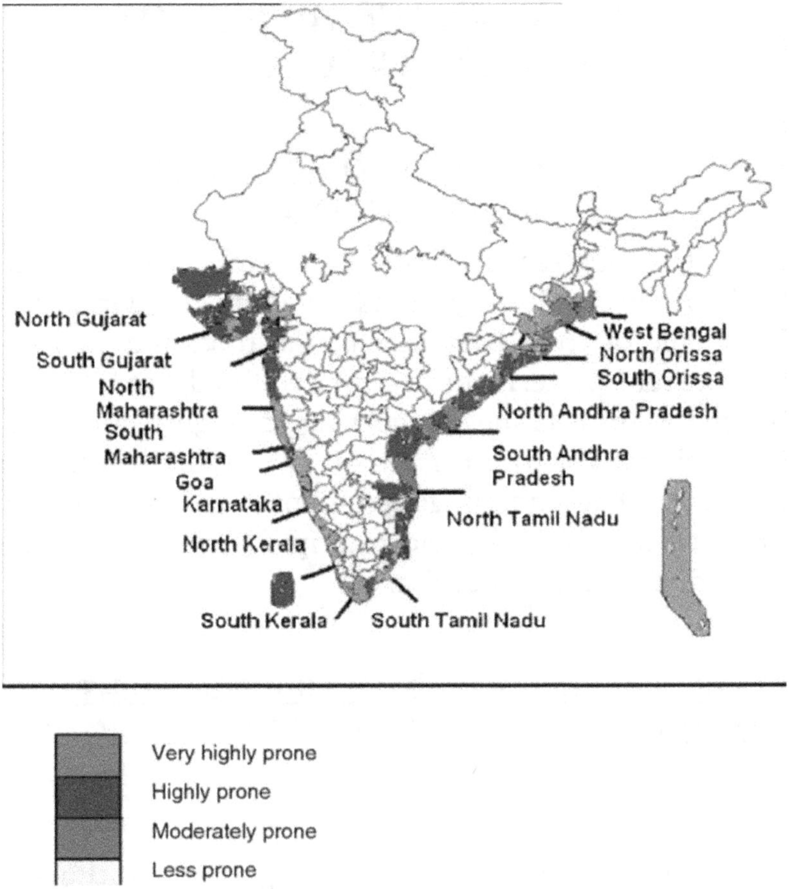

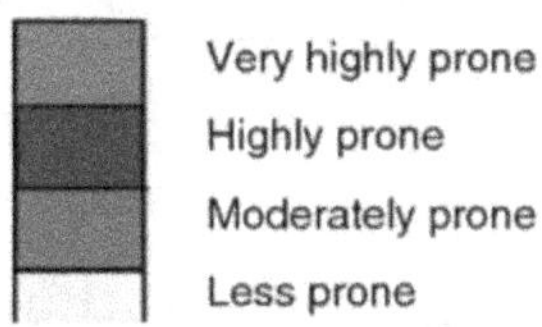

ADAPTATION AND MITIGATION OF CLIMATE CHANGE

INDIANSTEPSTO MITIGATE THE CLIMATICCHANGES

Thus the process of global warming has affected India intensely, destroying its economy and depriving its people of their basic needs like food and shelter. The current patterns of destructive floods, increasing intensity of cyclones, recurring droughts and the increasing temperatures are all the results of global warming. The Indian governmental so realizes the predictament it faces, and multiple steps to mitigate these disasters have been taken.

STEPS TAKEN BY INDIAN GOVERNEMENT TO MITIGATE FLOODS AND OTHER CLIMATIC DISASTERS

In India, National Disaster Management Authority (NDMA) is the apex body for addressing the disaster related policy issues and for laying guidelines. The Ministry of Environment and Forests, the Ministry of Science and Technology, the Ministry of External

Affairs as well as the Prime Minister's Office are the offices related to climatic changes.

India has always been plagued by the recurrent and devastating floods. The history of mitigating steps taken by the Indian government can be traced back to1953, when the unprecedented floods of 1953 struck India, at which time the first national policy in thisregard was made. After that, every government employed many policies and committees to counteract the dreaded floodsand their devastations. Most notable of them were thefollowing.

- High level committee on floods-1957
- Policy statement on floods-1958
- Ministerial committee on flood control-1964
- Minister's committee on flood and flood relief 1972
- Working group on flood control for five year plans
- National Flood Commission-1980
- National water policy-1987
- National commission for integrated water resource development plan-1996
- Five regional task forces-1996

COMMUNITY BASED DISASTER PREPAREDNESS (CBDP)

The ministry of Home Affairs, government of India has taken an initiative at local level

Known as the community based disaster preparedness. It functions with the help of the local people as well as the NGOs to help prepare the people for different climatic disasters by mobilizing them easily, and helping in providing relief to the affected community. Other tasks of this committee include the preparation of seasonal calendars to predict the climatic disasters, mapping the risks faced by the community and taking actions to prevent them.

STEPS REQUIRED BY THE INDIAN GOVERNMENT TO MITIGATE GLOBAL WARMING AND RESULTING CLIMATIC DIASTERS

In spite of the steps taken by the Indian government, global warming continues to increase, and the resulting climatic disasters ravage the country in an unabated manner. This can be attributed to the lack of resources, and access to technology. To cope up with the climate change-disasters-security nexus, the country needs to have a better technical understanding, capacity building, networking and expansive consultation processes spanning every section of the society.

The committees and organizations working to counteract against the climatic disasters work independently from each other. The ongoing climatic changes, with an increase in a possibility of more disasters impose imperatives for a unity among all these bodies, resulting in an integrated risk management framework, creating a common platform for the committees to work on.

India has a distinctive vulnerability profile as the poor are the most affected. Tremendous weather events take place more frequently and are becoming more ruthless. Therefore the previous attempts of just rescuing the affected will not be enough now, instead, meticulous steps to prevent these disasters are required. This can only be met if the strategies and policies can cope with climate change, requiring the active participation of the government and the people.

Primary data

Bihar

Sushant panday
from South Bihar

According to him Bihar has two climatic conditions. One is North Bihar which is vulnerable to floods. The river Koshi is called sorrow of Bihar because of its

floods.
And second one is South Bihar where drought is seen. In current year 2022 the late in monsoon disturbed the crops and rain in September October months and in winters creates difficult condition for Kharif crops
All these situations like change in rain pattern with respect to months and places are direct examples of climate change.

Ashutosh Kumar
North Bihar

North Bihar faces floods every year. This is not because the government is not taking steps but the untimely rains and the Himalayan rivers like Koshi, Gandak, Budhi Gandak are bringing flash floods suddenly. In recent years this is seen very often. This may be because of the melting of glaciers and because of which Himalayan rivers are full of water.
Apart from this he says the floods in winters makes situation very challenging and this is the direct impact of climate change.

Uttrakhand
Subhash mehra

Subhash says he lives in hilly areas. The graphical conditions are never good to live but in recent years landslide incidents are increased. He further added that the temperature in the summer is also raised in recent years, which is directly linked with the landslides. According to Subhash this is the first direct impact of climate change on human. Hilly terrains are the most vulnerable to climate change.

Ladakh
Tshring
From Leh

Tshring belongs to Leh and his family is basically sheep farmers. He says that it is seen that in these days snow fall Stops early and ice melts early because of this our sheep gets grass but the rivers which are basically glacier dependent are shortage of water for a long time in the year. Thus climate change creates different and difficult situations for them.

West Bengal
Subhodip mandal

Subhodip says his state is located near the Bay of Bengal thus cyclones with heavy storm and winds are seen there. He says his grandmother was saying that cyclones were not that frequent like recent years. Now 2-3 cyclones are seen in Bay of Bengal during summer only. Subhodip further added that this is directly linked with the climate change. As cyclones are formed due to heating of sea water (21°C), rising the global temperature with global warming made it very common.

Arif Ahmed

Arif remembers the super cyclone Amphan witch hit the West Bengal in 2020. He says the wind speed was so high that damaged lots of building and house in coastal areas.

Jharkhand
Rohit saw

Rohit says about the crop pattern which is directly disturbed by the climate change in Jharkhand. In 2022 monsoon was very weak in the starting two months because of which Jharkhand government published a list of district facing drought situation but in later months the monsoon rain very much and those districts are facing high rain situation. But ultimately crop pattern disturbed and farmers of Jharkhand faced problems.

Amit kumar
Amit is from western part of Jharkhand with is geographically call Pat area of Jharkhand because of the hilly and down terrain. Amit says in last five years only two years were good for agriculture and for three years they can't get any crop for the fields because of less rainfall.

Karnataka
Kamdev singh
Kamdev works in Bengaluru he pointed the recent flood situation in Bengaluru because of heavy rain. He added this are the impact of climate change only.

Gujarat

Kumud patel

Kumud says in 2021 cyclone Tauktae hit the Gujarat and Maharastra coast. Kumud is a Geography graduate so he elaborate the point that the Arabian sea region and the west coast of India gets less cyclone because the temperature of the Arabian sea is low and cyclones need high sea water temperature but as the global temperature is rising because of green house gases, west coast is also getting lots of cyclones and this is not a good sign for India because the western part of India is the economic centre of entire country.

CHAPTER-5 : INDIA'S ACTION

Indias action against climate change

India's Climate Commitments: Paris Agreement and Beyond

India has made significant pledges under the Paris Agreement, aiming to reduce greenhouse gas emissions, increase the use of renewable energy, and strengthen resilience to climate change. These commitments are outlined in India's Nationally Determined Contributions (NDC), which were first submitted in 2015 and have been updated periodically to reflect evolving targets.

NDC Commitments-

a. Emissions Intensity Reduction: India committed to reducing the emissions intensity of its GDP (emissions per unit of economic output) by 33-35% by 2030, compared to 2005 levels. This is a significant pledge considering India's rapidly growing economy.
b. Renewable Energy Capacity: India has set an ambitious goal to achieve 500 GW of non-fossil fuel-based energy capacity by 2030. This includes a massive scale-up in solar and

wind power.

c. Forest and Tree Cover: India aims to increase its forest cover to absorb more carbon. The goal is to create an additional 2.5 to 3 billion tons of CO2 equivalent of carbon sink by increasing green cover, including through afforestation and reforestation initiatives.

India's Role in Global Conferences:

COP26 (Glasgow, 2021): India played a key role in negotiations at COP26, where it announced more ambitious climate targets. Prime Minister Modi unveiled India's "Panchamrit" or five key climate goals for 2030, which include:

a. Reaching net-zero emissions by 2070.
b. Increasing renewable energy capacity to 500 GW.
c. Reducing emissions intensity by 45% by 2030 compared to 2005 levels.
d. Achieving 50% of total energy from renewables.
e. Increasing carbon sink through afforestation and restoration of ecosystems.

COP27 (Sharm El-Sheikh, 2022)- India continued to stress the need for developed countries to honor their climate finance commitments and called for greater action on loss and damage caused by climate change. India emphasized that climate justice must be at the heart of global climate action, advocating for fairer responsibility-sharing between developed and developing nations.

Renewable Energy Expansion-

India has made tremendous progress in expanding renewable energy capacity, with solar and wind power leading the charge, complemented by a growing focus on other renewable sources.

Solar Power- India has one of the most ambitious solar energy targets in the world. Under its National Solar Mission, India aims to achieve 280 GW of solar capacity by 2030. Bhadla Solar Park in Rajasthan is a symbol of India's commitment to solar energy. With a capacity of 2,245 MW, it is the largest solar park in the world. India has been scaling up its rooftop solar initiative and investing in solar-powered irrigation systems, especially in rural areas. The development of solar-plus-storage systems is seen as crucial to managing intermittent solar power generation. Wind Energy:India is also a global leader in wind energy. It has set a target of 140 GW of wind capacity by 2030. Coastal States: States like Tamil Nadu and Gujarat have been pioneers in wind energy development, with Tamil Nadu alone contributing nearly 40% of India's total wind energy capacity. Offshore wind energy is also gaining attention, with plans to harness the potential off the coast of Gujarat. Other Renewable Energy Sources: Bioenergy: India is expanding its bioenergy capacity, focusing on biogas and biomass power generation. The Pradhan Mantri Ujjwala Yojana aims to provide clean cooking fuel to millions of rural households, reducing the reliance on traditional biomass for cooking. Geothermal and Tidal Energy: Although still in early stages, India is exploring the potential of geothermal energy (especially in states like Himachal Pradesh and Jammu & Kashmir) and tidal energy along its long coastline.

Challenges and Achievements-

Grid Integration : A major challenge is integrating the growing renewable capacity with the national grid, particularly solar and wind, which are variable in nature. Energy Storage: To overcome intermittency, India is investing in energy storage solutions like batteries and pumped hydro storage. India has made impressive strides in reducing the cost of renewable energy, making it one of the most cost-competitive countries for solar and wind power.

Sustainable Agriculture and Water Management

Agriculture is a critical sector for India's economy and its population. With changing rainfall patterns and increasing temperatures, India has been focusing on climate-resilient agriculture and sustainable water use.

Climate-Resilient Agriculture : India is promoting climate-resilient agriculture practices that can withstand the adverse effects of climate change, including shifting weather patterns, droughts, and floods. Organic Farming: Programs like the National

Mission on Sustainable Agriculture (NMSA) encourage organic farming, reducing dependence on chemical fertilizers and promoting soil health.

Diversified Crops : India is promoting the cultivation of climate-appropriate, less resource-intensive crops, such as millets, which require less water and are more drought-resistant compared to traditional crops like rice.

Water Management : Water is a critical resource, and efficient water use is essential for sustainable farming in India. Pradhan Mantri Krishi Sinchai Yojana (PMKSY)-This scheme aims to improve irrigation efficiency and ensure that every farm has access to water through efficient irrigation systems. It promotes the adoption of micro-irrigation techniques like drip and sprinkler irrigation, which reduce water wastage and improve crop yields.

Watershed Management : Various programs focus on rejuvenating watersheds and improving the management of groundwater resources in water-scarce regions.

Few examples are In Maharashtra, the government has implemented water-saving techniques, including rainwater harvesting and small-scale water storage systems, to combat droughts and ensure water availability for irrigation. And Zero Budget Natural Farming (ZBNF) in states like Andhra Pradesh has gained popularity for its focus on low-cost, low-input sustainable farming practices that prioritize natural fertilizers, water efficiency, and reduced carbon emissions.

Electric Mobility and Transportation Reforms

Transportation is a major source of greenhouse gas emissions in India, making it a crucial area for climate action. The Indian government has rolled out various initiatives to promote electric vehicles (EVs), reduce dependence on fossil fuels, and improve air quality.

Government Policies and Incentives : Faster Adoption and Manufacturing of Hybrid and Electric Vehicles : Launched in 2015, the FAME scheme is a flagship government initiative to promote the adoption of electric and hybrid vehicles in India. It provides financial incentives for the purchase of electric two-wheelers, three-wheelers, buses, and cars, as well as funding for EV charging infrastructure. FAME II (2019-2022) further expanded the incentives, with an increased focus on public transport (electric buses) and the establishment of a robust charging infrastructure. GST Reduction: The Indian government has reduced the Goods and Services Tax (GST) on electric vehicles to 5%, compared to 28% for conventional vehicles, making EVs more affordable.

Investment in EV Infrastructure : The government has committed to the creation of an EV charging network to support the growing number of electric vehicles. The National Electric Mobility Mission Plan (NEMMP) aims to set up charging stations at regular intervals on major highways and urban areas. Private sector investments in battery manufacturing are also expanding, with companies like Tata Motors and Mahindra Electric focusing on local manufacturing of electric cars, buses, and batteries to reduce costs and dependence on imports. Battery swapping stations are being piloted in cities like Delhi and Bengaluru as part of an effort to make EVs more accessible, particularly for two-wheelers and three-wheelers.

Sustainable Transport Initiatives : In urban areas, India is promoting the use of public transport systems to reduce traffic congestion and emissions. Cities like Delhi, Mumbai, and Bengaluru are expanding their metro networks and bus rapid transit systems (BRTS). Electric buses are being introduced in many cities, with the government aiming to deploy 5,000 electric buses by 2030. The Delhi Metro is a key example of India's commitment to cleaner, sustainable transport. The Delhi Metro Rail Corporation (DMRC) is working towards becoming carbon-neutral by 2030. The DMRC has incorporated solar power generation at its stations and depots and aims to meet 30% of its energy needs through renewable sources. The Metro is also integrating electric buses into its transport network, further reducing emissions from public transport.

Forestry and Biodiversity Conservation

Forestry and biodiversity conservation are essential to India's climate strategy, as forests play a crucial role in carbon sequestration, while biodiversity helps build ecosystem resilience to climate change.

Green India Mission :

The Green India Mission (GIM), launched in 2014 as part of India's National Action Plan on Climate Change (NAPCC), aims to enhance carbon sinks through afforestation and improving forest quality. The mission targets increasing forest and tree cover by 5 million hectares by 2030 and increasing the forest-based livelihood of communities. It emphasizes sustainable management of forests and aims to increase the carbon stock in forests.

Community-led Conservation :

Joint Forest Management (JFM) initiatives involve local communities in the protection and management of forests, providing them with sustainable livelihoods while enhancing forest regeneration and biodiversity.

Several projects promote biodiversity conservation, including efforts to protect the Western Ghats and the Sundarbans mangroves, which are both rich in biodiversity and crucial for carbon storage.

Mangrove Restoration :

Mangrove restoration projects have gained traction, especially in coastal areas vulnerable to climate change. India's mangrove ecosystems, particularly in states like West Bengal, Gujarat, and Odisha, are vital in protecting coastal communities from sea-level rise, storms, and erosion.

Mangrove forests also act as important carbon sinks, and efforts to restore them are aligned with India's broader climate goals.

Challenges in Balancing Conservation and Development :

One of the key challenges in forestry conservation is balancing forest protection with the need for land for economic development, particularly in tribal and rural areas. There is a need to ensure that conservation initiatives do not displace local communities or hinder their access to forest resources.

Land-use changes, such as for infrastructure projects, often result in deforestation, making it crucial to have policies that promote sustainable land management.

Climate-Resilient Urbanization and Infrastructure

As India's urban population grows, building climate-resilient cities becomes increasingly important. The focus is on reducing urban vulnerability to climate change, improving infrastructure, and promoting sustainable urban development.

Green Infrastructure :

The Smart Cities Mission, launched in 2015, aims to transform Indian cities into sustainable, inclusive, and resilient urban spaces. The mission focuses on the use of green technologies, including energy-efficient lighting, water conservation, and renewable energy integration.

Indian cities are investing in green infrastructure such as urban parks, green roofs, and rainwater harvesting systems to improve the environmental quality of urban spaces while mitigating the impacts of climate change.

Green Building Standards- The government has adopted green building standards like IGBC (Indian Green Building Council) and LEED (Leadership in Energy and Environmental Design) to encourage energy-efficient construction in urban areas.

Policies are being implemented to promote sustainable building materials and energy-efficient design in both new developments and renovations of existing infrastructure.

Flood Control and Climate Adaptation :

Cities like Bengaluru and Chennai are implementing flood-control measures such as rainwater harvesting systems, better stormwater drainage networks, and wetland restoration.

The government is also focusing on developing climate-adaptive urban planning, ensuring that cities are prepared to handle extreme weather events, such as floods, heatwaves, and droughts, which are becoming more frequent due to climate change.

Climate Financing and Green Economy Transition

India's ambitious climate goals require significant financial resources. The Indian government, in collaboration with international bodies, is working to mobilize climate financing to support the transition to a green economy.

Role in the Green Climate Fund :

India is an active participant in the Green Climate Fund (GCF), which aims to assist developing countries in mitigating and adapting to climate change. India has secured funding from the GCF for several renewable energy and adaptation projects.

India's National Adaptation Fund for Climate Change (NAFCC) provides financial support for projects focused on improving climate resilience, especially in vulnerable regions.

Government-led Green Bonds :

India has issued green bonds to raise funds for projects in renewable energy, energy efficiency, and sustainable infrastructure. The Indian government is also offering financial incentives for companies and individuals to invest in green technologies and low-carbon projects.

Public-Private Partnerships :

Public-private partnerships (PPPs) are crucial for scaling up investment in renewable energy and climate mitigation. India has attracted significant private sector investment in solar and wind energy, as well as in sustainable urban infrastructure and electric mobility projects.

Barriers and Opportunities :

Barriers: Despite these efforts, scaling up climate financing faces several challenges, including policy uncertainty, lack of financial incentives for private sector investment, and a shortage of local financial instruments to support green projects.

Opportunities: There is significant potential for expanding blended finance models, which combine public and private funding, as well as increasing international climate finance to support India's energy transition and climate adaptation projects.

Public Awareness and Grassroots Initiatives

Public awareness and grassroots initiatives are essential in shaping the success of climate action policies, particularly in a diverse and populous country like India. By empowering communities and fostering environmental consciousness, India has made significant strides in involving the public in efforts to combat climate change.

Role of NGOs, Civil Society, and Educational Programs

Non-governmental organizations (NGOs), civil society groups, and educational programs have been pivotal in raising climate awareness and promoting sustainable practices across India. These organizations play a crucial role in disseminating information, educating communities, and building a climate-resilient society.

NGOs and Civil Society : In India, NGOs have long been at the forefront of environmental activism, providing the backbone for grassroots mobilization. Organizations like The Energy and Resources Institute (TERI), Centre for Science and Environment (CSE), and Greenpeace India have been instrumental in raising awareness about issues such as air pollution, deforestation, water conservation, and climate change. These groups conduct research, create awareness campaigns, and engage in lobbying efforts to influence policy decisions.

Campaigns and Education : NGOs often work with schools and local communities to conduct educational campaigns. Programs like "Mission 1 Million", led by TERI, are designed to educate school children about the importance of sustainability. Similarly, grassroots movements like Jhatka vs. Lasso and Chal Rang De (a campaign for solar energy adoption) focus on encouraging individuals to adopt clean energy practices.

Government-Supported Educational Programs : The Indian government, through programs like the National Action Plan on Climate Change (NAPCC) and Swachh Bharat Mission, has promoted the integration of climate change education into school curricula, aiming to instill a sense of environmental responsibility from an early age.

Community-Led Initiatives for Renewable Energy, Waste Management, and Afforestation

Grassroots communities are increasingly taking charge of their environmental futures by initiating local-level projects to address climate-related challenges.

Renewable Energy Adoption : India has seen a surge in community-led solar energy projects. Rural areas, often far from the grid, are benefiting from decentralized renewable energy solutions. For example, the Barefoot College in Rajasthan trains women in rural communities to install and maintain solar panels. These initiatives not only provide access to renewable energy but also empower communities economically by creating jobs in the renewable sector.

Waste Management Initiatives : Local communities have become integral to India's waste management revolution. Projects like Kamraj Nagar in Chennai, which adopted segregated waste collection and composting, and "Zero Waste" communities in Pune and Bengaluru, emphasize the importance of recycling and composting. Through these initiatives, residents are educated on the need to reduce plastic use, compost organic waste, and recycle materials like paper and metal.

Afforestation Projects : Grassroots efforts are critical in India's push for afforestation and forest conservation. Initiatives like The Chipko Movement (which began in Uttarakhand) have been pivotal in engaging local communities, especially women, in protecting forests from deforestation. In recent years, several local movements have emerged to plant trees, protect biodiversity, and combat soil erosion. In Madhya Pradesh, community-driven Van Samitis (forest councils) work to protect forest resources and engage in activities such as tree planting and forest regeneration.

The Influence of Movements like Swachh Bharat on Environmental Consciousness

The Swachh Bharat Abhiyan, launched in 2014, has played a transformative role in changing the mindset of the Indian public toward sanitation and waste management, with an eventual environmental benefit. Initially focused on the goal of a "clean India," the mission has since evolved to encourage practices that reduce environmental degradation. It promotes practices like segregation of waste, composting, and plastic-free initiatives.

The success of Swachh Bharat's awareness campaigns has also sparked local initiatives that go beyond cleanliness to include water conservation, air pollution control, and the reduction of single-use plastics. Swachh Bharat has fostered an environmental consciousness in both urban and rural areas, resulting in a more engaged citizenry in climate action.

Notable Grassroots Environmentalists and Their Contributions

Several grassroots environmentalists have made remarkable contributions to environmental protection, including :

Rajendra Singh (Waterman of India): Rajendra Singh is a well-known environmentalist from Rajasthan who has dedicated his life to the conservation of water. He revitalized the Arvari River by organizing communities to clean and restore the river and develop rainwater harvesting systems in drought-prone regions.

Medha Patkar (Narmada Bachao Andolan) : Medha Patkar led the Narmada Bachao Andolan (Save Narmada Movement), a successful protest against the building of large dams on the Narmada River. She brought attention to the environmental and social impacts of large-scale infrastructure projects, advocating for sustainable water management practices.

Madhav Gadgi l: An environmental scientist who played

a pivotal role in the formation of the Western Ghats Ecology Expert Panel, Madhav Gadgil's work in the Western Ghats region helped raise awareness about the threats to biodiversity in the ecologically sensitive area.

Climate Adaptation Strategies for Vulnerable Communities

India's vulnerability to climate change is particularly high in rural, coastal, and tribal regions, where communities are already experiencing severe impacts such as droughts, floods, and extreme heat. Adaptation strategies are vital to building resilience in these areas.

Supporting Farmers and Rural Communities

Farmers, especially small-scale farmers, are facing increasingly erratic weather patterns, such as delayed monsoons, droughts, and floods. Adapting agriculture to these changing conditions is crucial.

Climate-Resilient Crops and Seeds : Programs like the National Mission for Sustainable Agriculture (NMSA) focus on promoting the use of climate-resilient seeds that are drought-resistant or flood-resistant, such as drought-tolerant rice and flood-resistant paddy varieties.

Crop Insurance : The Pradhan Mantri Fasal Bima Yojana (PMFBY) is a government scheme that provides insurance cover to farmers against weather-related crop losses. This program aims to help farmers cope with financial losses caused by climate-induced disasters.

Water Management : Projects like micro-irrigation systems, including drip irrigation and rainwater harvesting in drought-prone areas, are helping farmers reduce water consumption and improve crop yields in the face of changing rainfall patterns.

Coastal Communities and Sea-Level Rise Adaptation

India's extensive coastline is highly vulnerable to the impacts of climate change, particularly sea-level rise and cyclones. Adaptation strategies focus on protecting these communities from climate impacts.

Seawalls and Coastal Protection : Seawalls and revetments are being constructed in several coastal states to protect communities from erosion and storm surges. For example, in Gujarat, the construction of coastal embankments helps protect vital infrastructure and agricultural land from sea intrusion.

Mangrove Restoration : Mangroves provide a natural barrier against storms and act as carbon sinks. The Sunderbans in West Bengal and Gulf of Kutch in Gujarat are examples where mangrove restoration has been prioritized to protect coastal areas from rising sea levels and increasing cyclone intensity.

Tribal Populations and Climate Resilience

Tribal communities are particularly vulnerable to climate change, as they often live in remote areas with limited access to healthcare, information, and resources.

Forest Conservation: Many tribal communities have been involved in community-led forest conservation efforts that both protect the environment and provide them with sustainable livelihoods.

Livelihood Diversification : Government programs like the National Rural Livelihood Mission (NRLM) focus on diversifying the income sources of tribal communities through skill development in areas like handicrafts, agroforestry, and ecotourism.

Challenges in Ensuring Equity in Adaptation Policies

A significant challenge in adaptation policy is ensuring that it is equitable and inclusive. Often, marginalized groups, including women, tribal communities, and lower-income households, are disproportionately affected by climate change, yet their needs are frequently overlooked in policy development.

Policies must integrate local knowledge, cultural practices, and gender-sensitive approaches to ensure that adaptation strategies are fair and effective for all members of society.

Technological Innovations in Climate Action

India is leveraging technology and innovation to address climate change challenges, and climate-tech startups are emerging as key players in the battle against global warming.

Technologies for Climate Mitigation and Adaptation

AI and Big Data in Agriculture : Innovations like precision agriculture, using AI and data analytics, are helping farmers adapt to climate change. AI models predict crop yields, monitor soil health, and optimize water usage, which helps reduce climate-induced agricultural losses.

Smart Energy Grids : The transition to smart grids is vital for integrating renewable energy into the power system. Smart grids can manage the fluctuating supply of renewable energy, improve energy efficiency, and reduce carbon emissions.

Satellite-Based Weather Forecasting : Technologies like satellite-based remote sensing and weather forecasting tools help predict extreme weather events like cyclones, floods, and droughts. This data is crucial for early warning systems and emergency preparedness.

Government Support for Research and Development

The Indian government supports climate-friendly technologies through funding mechanisms like National Clean Energy Fund (NCEF), Clean Development Mechanism (CDM), and the Technology Development and Demonstration Program (TDDP), which promote innovation in clean energy and sustainable technologies.

International Collaborations and India's Global Role

India has played a leading role in global climate discussions, advocating for climate equity, and engaging in international partnerships.

India's Leadership in Global Initiatives

International Solar Alliance (ISA) : Launched by India and France, the ISA aims to promote solar energy and ensure that affordable and clean energy reaches countries in the Global South. By harnessing solar potential across the world, India has positioned itself as a leader in the transition to renewable energy.

Technology Transfer and Capacity Building

India is collaborating with developed countries to gain access to climate technologies and build local capacities in climate mitigation and adaptation strategies. This includes joint ventures in solar energy, electric mobility, and energy efficiency projects.

Climate Equity Advocacy

India has long advocated for climate equity in international climate talks, pushing for developed nations to take responsibility for historical emissions and provide financing for developing countries to tackle climate change. India's stance on common but differentiated responsibilities (CBDR) has been a key theme in negotiations at UNFCCC and COP summits.

Challenges and Criticisms in India's Climate Policy

India's climate policies face significant challenges, particularly regarding balancing economic growth with environmental sustainability.

Economic Growth vs. Climate Goals

Industrialization : India's rapid industrialization and need for economic development often conflict with climate targets. Reliance on coal for power generation remains high, making it challenging to cut emissions.

Fossil Fuel Dependency : Despite renewable energy growth, India remains one of the world's largest consumers of coal. This is a point of criticism for environmental groups, who argue that the country's future energy transition needs to be more ambitious.

Social Issues : Displacement from renewable energy projects and impacts on local communities are additional concerns. Large-scale solar and wind farms can sometimes displace communities or lead to land-use conflicts, requiring more inclusive planning.

The Road Ahead : Future Strategies and Goals

India has set ambitious goals for a net-zero emissions future by 2070, including key milestones like 50% energy from renewables by 2030 and a 30-35% reduction in emissions intensity by 2030.

Key Areas for Focus :

Energy Storage and Hydrogen : As renewable energy penetration grows, energy storage solutions like battery storage and hydrogen energy will be critical to ensure grid stability.

Youth Engagement : Youth-driven movements like Fridays for Future are mobilizing support for greater climate action, highlighting the importance of involving younger generations in policymaking.

Innovative Approaches :

India's future climate strategy will rely on innovation, collaboration, and policy reforms, positioning India as a key player in global efforts to combat climate change while balancing economic development and sustainability.

CHAPTER-6 : CONCLUSIONS AND SUGGESTIONS

CONCLUSION AND SUGGESTIONS

The multiplicity of causes makes it difficult to clearly delineate the causes and consequences of environmental degradation in terms of simple one to one relationship. The causes and effects are often interwoven in complex webs of social, technological, environmental and political factors. However, some of the very common causes of global warming which can be clearly pointed are the pollution, greenhouse effect, solar radiation, deforestation, industrialization population growth, the economic growth associated with the affluence factor and change of technology.

In view of the position stated aforesaid, the problem of global warming has posed new challenges. This requires not only a careful and cautious handling of the problem under consideration but also requires a meticulous approach to tackle it more effectively and in a planned manner. In other words, it becomes essential that we formulate policies both at the national and the international level for protecting the environment and conserving it for a better tomorrow.

Population is an important resource for development, yet it is a major cause of environmental degradation when it exceeds the threshold limits of the support system. The process of development itself also leads to damage of the environment if not properly managed. Associated with the rapid economic growth, the extravagant affluence consumes far more resources and put far greater pressure on natural resources.

The change of technology causes planned obsolescence causing the generation of more and more wastes which in turn prove ecologically harmful. Short-term interests of private profit maximization further hamper the process of replacement of absolute technologies by the ecologically benign technologies.

In addition to the above factors, the political factors also contribute to environmental degradation. In a democratic polity like India, governments frequently adopt short-term measures unmindful of their long-term impacts. Incremental decision- making that most closely approximate the status quo is useful for a government that must win a not too distant election. Consequently, short-term stability is prime while long-term stability and welfare are at a discount. In such a system it is difficult to persuade a government to take unpopular measures that would benefit future generations and strengthen the long-term stability of society.

Likewise the multiplicity of pollutants differing in their composition behaviour, manner of their entry into the environment and our lack of knowledge of fundamental aspects of biosphere make the determination of sources of environmental degradation still more difficult, complex and subtle task. The sources of global warming are many and overlapping, ranging from natural to man made. Many of the latter sources cannot be subjected to regulation or to preventive measures. However, from the protective perspective the following categories of sources can be considered as threatening for global warming:

(a) Water pollution by industries and municipalities,
(b) Air pollution by industrial units and vehicles,
(b) Environmental degradation due to the excessive use of insecticides and fertilizers,
(c) steady and gradual depletion of the non-renewable resources,
(e) Degradation of land because of deforestation and
(f) Haphazard urban growth.

All the above sources are self-explanatory and continue to cause global warming. The consequences of the effects of global warming are numerous. These global warming sources also have the social implications and they affect various human rights namely right to life, right to health, right to water, right to livelihood, right of self- determination also global warming vulnerabilities are more to the specific groups like children, women, tribal people etc.

Despite existence of Environmental Policy, the constitutional mandate of environmental protection flurry of legislations and administrative infrastructure of implementation the fact remains that problem of global warming still remains a great cause of concern in our country. The unabated deterioration of environmental quality most vividly reflects the failure of the earlier environmental policy and of the legislative and administrative initiatives taken to improve or conserve environment. Failure to achieve desired results even after over two decades of adoption of environmental protection measures reflects incompatibility of the policy resolutions and the legal mechanism. Deterioration of environment cannot be allowed to perpetuate. Prudent environment management is the need of hour. Sound environment management which essentially involves optional allocation of finite resources between different possible uses, is so complex that suggesting any particular solution would not in itself be self- sufficient. However, a few suggestions relating to planning and for improvement of legal as well as enforcement mechanism may be given here which if operationalized may prove relevant and viable to lessen the pollution problems.

A. Environmental Planning

It is acknowledged fact that environmental planning process has to set policies, priorities and techniques in such a manner that it can be readily reoriented and understood on a system of feedback system. Equally important is that environmental planning need to be devised in such a way that it attempts to facilitate economic development, avoiding, as far as possible or maintaining certainly concomitant environmental damage. It is heartening to note that Government of India has now come forward with a firm commitment to save and improve environment. In pursuance of this commitment it has formulated a new environmental policy which envisages comprehensive action programs and strategies for combating pollution problems. The strategy, on the paper at least looks quite impressive touching upon every environmental component. The policy objectives are still in the initial stage of implementation. Therefore, pollution abatement efforts can make their impact felt only over a long period of time. At the same time, the policy suffers from some apparent defects which need to be removed for its smooth operationalization. The following suggestions may prove fruitful in removing the defects of the policy.

(a) Inclusion of Environmental protection in Concurrent List

It is known that a majority of environment related subjects fall within the legislative competence of State Legislatures. Therefore the success of new environmental policy will largely depend upon how fairly and sincerely states implement the policy objectives or the suggested strategies incorporated therein. To bypass the federal versus state dichotomy in implementation of policy objectives it is suggested that environment protection may be included in the concurrent list, in seventh schedule of the Constitution so as to enable the central government to effectively take appropriate steps to put strategies of environment protection into action as and when the need to do so arises.

(b) Removal of Inter-Policy Conflicts

It has been seen that despite the mandate. of the new environmental policy to integrate and internalize environmental considerations in the policies and programmes of development in various sectors, inter-policy conflicts cannot be overruled in the absence of any coordinator and supervising body to look into the compliance of the objective. New economic policy is one example of such inter-policy conflicts which has been adopted without enough environmental impacts being taken into consideration or even the Ministry of Environment being consulted. It is, therefore, desirable that the Ministry of Environment be designated as a coordinating and supervisory institution to ensure that environmental considerations are not only incorporated in other policy statements but put into action with due regard to environmental safeguards.

(c) Devising Policies for Uncovered Areas of Environment Protection

It is a sad affair that despite devising a new environmental policy, there are certain areas of environment protection which still remain uncovered. We don't have any policy on Municipal Waste Management in spite of the fact that eighty per cent of the entire pollution load comes from the municipal wastes. Collection, transportation and safe disposal of wastes is the biggest problem despoiling the urban environment. The most obvious consequences of this problem are the prevailing inhuman conditions and outbreak of epidemics in our cities and towns. The recent outbreak of plague in Surat and other parts of the country is just one example of appalling insanitary conditions in our country which has injured our national pride overseas. This state of affairs reflects individuals' indifference and the casual attitude of the administration to community hygiene. In the backdrop of the prevailing situation, it is high time that citizens become more aware of civic sense and be assertive and demanding to put authorities on their toes to ensure the evolution of a system of accountability in relation to efficient management of dirt and filth. This is the only way to check the bureaucrats who harp on the 'steps taken' on public matters, including ever mounting heaps of garbage. This can only discipline our indifferent politicians who add to slum infused dirt and fifth or embark upon short-term ecologically harmful developmental plans for vote catching. It is equally important at the same time that Government of India comes forward with a comprehensive solid Waste Management plan at the national level providing for effective collection, transportation, disposal and recycling of waste materials. Necessary infrastructure and adequate finances be created for this purpose.

(d) Adoption of Improved Policy Instruments

The instruments for achievement of environmental policy objectives being employed also suffer from many deficiencies. They need to be mended for effective implementation.

B. Legal Enforcement Machinery

Legislation and policy pronouncements will be ineffective as long as the enforcement machinery remains week. Therefore, a fresh look is desired on strengthening the enforcement mechanism. The following suggestions in this regard may be considered for implementation.

(a) Structural Changes in the Enforcement Agencies

Bureaucratization of agencies responsible for control of pollution such as the local self-governmental bodies and Pollution Control Boards is a great malady of Indian pollution control mechanism. Democratisation of these bodies or agencies with the involvement of people having interest and expertise in environment protection is the only method of activating the environment mandate. The Constitution of such bodies need to be restructured to enable participation of scientists, ecologists, environmentalists, sociologists, economists and lawyers. Doing such will bring in impartiality and efficiency in the working of these agencies Also, needed is coordination between these different bodies which can be brought in through allocation of defined functions avoiding overlapping. The Department of Environment or a specialized agency under its wing in each state may be given administrative control to ensure that coordination is maintained between the various bodies engaged in environment protection programmes.

(b) More Powers to Boards

With the recent amendments in the environment legislation, more administrative powers have been conferred on the Pollution Control Board. This step is welcome and is in the right direction. It will not be unsafe to give more powers to enforcing agencies which may include power to fine and secure convictions in case of violation of anti- pollution laws. Combining administrative powers as well as judicial powers in one body may be objected to on the ground that the same body will be prosecutor and a judge. Such combination of functions has been safely employed in our legal system. However to avoid such a situation, a separate legal cell may be created within the enforcing institution which may be entrusted with the legal functions while administrative wing may be entrusted with monitoring and enforcement of regulations. It may be added here that in addition to conferring more powers on the enforcement authorities, there is a need of fixing accountability of these bodies by statute, in order to promote their operational functioning. Mandatory duties may be imposed on local authorities or other bodies to ensure that they enforce pollution laws. A provision for personal liability of officer or officers for neglect of such duties may be provided for. There should also be a separate pollution control cell established in each of the municipalities.

(c) Environmental Courts

Environmental litigation, keeping in view its complex nature and the necessity of speedier justice should be adjudicated by multidisciplinary courts. Environmental courts may be set up in each state and union territories with an appellant court at the center. The court should consist of at least 3 member judges of which one should be man having necessary expertise in environmental sciences. The courts should have jurisdiction to decide all civil cases of compensation for the alleged injury which may be caused by environmental degradation. All public spirited individuals or groups should have direct access to such courts in bringing an action. These courts should be free to evolve their own procedures and should have authority to give directions to or command information from administrative authorities or polluters.

(d) Public Participation

Environment protection programs and legislations are meaningless as long as the victims of pollution are denied participation in the process of law-making and implementation. Larger Public participation can solve much of the environmental management problems. Thus, the public must be allowed, when necessary to pursue consent, 'license or permit applications of prospective polluters join government officials in inspection of any premises or process indulging in polluting or hazardous activities file complaints against violators or afforestation or reclamation programmes. Information dissemination is crucial in order to generate capability in the citizens to enable such participation. The public participation should be in a true decentralized manner extended to individual as well as to group or co-operative level involving non-governmental organisations local bodies and Panchayats. Necessary aid-financial or legal or technical may be given to voluntary organisation or groups engaged in environment protection.

SUGGESTED STRATEGIES FOR ENVIRONMENT MANAGEMENT

Implementation of environmental protection laws is an area where legislative as well as curative approach is desirable. It has been seen in the preceding discussion that enforcement of criminal sanctions for protecting environment is a very complicated affair. In fact the adjudication of environmental cases demands expertise from different discipline and different methods. In fact no other form of legislative activity warrants such diverse approaches and methods and multidisciplinary evaluation as is required in environmental litigation. The resulting effect has been the failure of prosecutorial strategy as an effective weapon for checking environmental pollution. Therefore, the entire body of laws substantive and procedures need a fresh look in its application to environmental issues. In fact, the preventive perspective needs to be strengthened for combating pollution. In the following pages an attempt is made to suggest some of the parameters for further strengthening the existing mechanism for pollution control.

A. Consent Administration

Under the law, the consent of the Board is necessary for a new or altered outlet or for new discharge of pollutants etc. The Acts lay down that such a consent shall be deemed to have been given unconditionally on the expiry of a period of four months from the date of making application unless the consent is given or refused earlier. This implies that if the consent application is not decided within the prescribed period, it shall amount to a grant of implied consent. In this connection the position in English law may be referred to. The English law provides that if within the period of 3 months of the date of application the authority has neither given nor refused the consent the authority shall be deemed to have refused the consent. It is therefore, suggested that the English provisions should be incorporated into the Indian laws with an additional rider that the board should publish a notice of such application in a newspaper having circulation in the area to which the application relates.

B. Public Participation and Access to Information

Members of the public are the most affected victims

of pollution but their participation in the pollution control process is lacking in a developing country like India. In the United States there has been a wide public participation in management of the environment. If environment management is to be made effective, it must have a participative basis. Hence, access to the court must be made available not only to the groups but even to private individuals. Interestingly, the Environment (Protection) Act

1986 provides for public participation in environmental management Section 19(b) of the EPA lays down that any person who has given notice of not less than 60 days in the manner prescribed, of the alleged offence and of his intention to make a complaint to the Central Government or authority or officer authorized, may make a complaint to the court. This means that a private individual or group can also proceed against the guilty in a court of law. Though the provision is a welcome step in the right direction but its effect has been whittled down by the fact that the requirement of 60 days' notice for filing such a complaint has• virtually rendered this provision ineffective. To make public participation as a potent weapon for combating pollution, it is suggested that the provision should be suitably amended and the limit of 60 days should be done away with.

Public participation presupposes a good system of public information. The people must have a right to receive information or to have information access. They must have the means to know the reports, details and other information concerning environment pollution. Section 20 of the EPA certainly enables the people to receive such information. It is therefore expected that the provisions in question would go a long way in encouraging effective people participation in environmental management. Closely connected to public participation is the question of environmental awareness. All possible steps should be taken for promoting environmental literacy through schools and colleges popular science forum and mass media.

C. Development of Compensatory Jurisprudence

The time has come when we must shift the emphasis from being one of criminal liability to that of a liability in tort. In other words, the violation of environmental laws should be treated as tort rather than a crime. This will not only compensate the victim but would also have a discouraging effect on the polluter from continuing the violation except at the cost of naturalization of his excess profits due to violations of environmental laws. Fortunately the Supreme Court of India has developed the principle of strict civil liability in accidental cases arising from the activities involving hazardous substances in Delhi Gas Leak case. The principle of Ryland's vs. Fletcher which was being followed in India since 1866 has been replaced by more rational and relevant principle of strict liability. The court was quite emphatic in holding that the industry which engages itself in hazardous or dangerous activity owes an absolute duty to the community to conduct its affairs with the highest conduct of safety and to- compensate if harm is caused to someone due to accident. Developing the principle of compensatory jurisprudence the court held that financial incapacity will not be a ground of defense. Countering the argument that enforcing the principle of strict liability may prove counterproductive as it may lead to the closure of the industry. the court observed: " ... the measure of compensation in these kind of cases must be con-elated to the magnitude and capacity of the enterprise because such compensation must have deferent effect. The larger and more prosperous the enterprise the greater must be the amount of compensation payable by it." It is submitted that the principle of compensation should be incorporated in the EPA 1986 by making suitable amendments. However, the Public Insurance Liability Act, 1991 has already incorporated this principle for measuring compensatory liability in accidental cases.

D. Need of Environmental Education

The seventies of the twentieth century will be known in the history of man as the decade of environmental revolution. The seventies started with the beginning of MAB program of the UNESCO, witnessed the United Nations Convergence on Human Environment (Stockholm, 1972), Human Settlements (Vancouver. 1976), Water (Mar del Pata, 1977), Desertification (Nairobi, 1977) UNEP-UNESCO Conference on Environmental Education (Tbilisi, 1977) and the UN

Conference on Science and Technology (Vienna, 1979). The question why environmental education has been discussed more than enough and the Governments as well as the individuals realize well the importance of Environmental Education is of great importance. The Environmental Education interest in recent years from both intra-curricular and extra-curricular point of view, although comparatively new, has been extremely keen and gathering momentum both within formal and non-formal systems.

BIBLIOGRAPHY

Secondary source

books

1. Agarwal, A., Narain, S., Sharma, A., & Imchen, A. (Eds.). (2001). *Green politics: Global environmental negotiation-2 (Poles apart)*. Centre for Science and Environment.

2. Agarwal, A., & Narain, S. (1991). *Global warming in an unequal world*. Centre for Science and Environment.

3. Agarwal, S. K. (2004). *Trade-related environmental measures in multilateral environmental agreements: A legal study*(Unpublished doctoral dissertation). Jawaharlal Nehru University.

4. Agarwal, A., Narain, S., & Sharma, A. (Eds.). (1999). *Green politics: Global environmental negotiation-1*. Centre for Science and Environment.

5. Agerup, M., & others. (Eds.). (2004). *Climate change and sustainable development: A blueprint from the Sustainable Development Network*. International Policy Network.

6. Aldy, J. E., Ashton, J., & others. (2003). *Beyond Kyoto: Advancing the international effort against climate change*. Pew Center for Global Climate Change.

7. Austin, D., & Faeth, P. (2000). *Financing sustainable development with the clean development mechanism*. World Resources Institute.

8. Barrett, S. (2003). *Environment & statecraft: The strategy of environmental treaty-making*. Oxford University Press.

9. Benedek, W. H. I., & Kicker, R. (Eds.). (1999). *Development and developing international and European law: Essays in honour of Kónrad Ginther*. Peter Lang.

10. Benedick, R. (1991). *Ozone diplomacy: New directions in safeguarding the planet*. Harvard University Press.

11. Desai, B. H. (2005). *Legal review of the basic framework of the 1992 UN Framework Convention on Climate Change, 1997 Kyoto Protocol, and intergovernmental negotiation process on global climate change*(Ministry of Environment & Forests Project Report). Jawaharlal Nehru University.

12. Pachauri, R. K., & Yogesh, K. (2018). *Renewable energy policy in India: Promises and challenges.*

Springer.

13. Gadgil, M., & Guha, R. (1993). *This fissured land: An ecological history of India.* Oxford University Press.

14. Dasgupta, P. (2021). *The economics of biodiversity: The Dasgupta review.* HM Treasury.

15. Srivastava, L., & Rehman, I. H. (2012). *Energy, environment, and development in India.* Routledge.

16. Gupta, J. (2014). *The history of global climate governance.* Cambridge University Press.

Government Reports

1. Ministry of Environment, Forest and Climate Change (MoEFCC). (2015). *India's Intended Nationally Determined Contributions (INDCs).* Official submission under the Paris Agreement outlining India's climate goals.
2. NITI Aayog. (2021). *India Energy Outlook 2021.* Provides insights into India's energy policies and their alignment with climate goals.
3. Ministry of New and Renewable Energy (MNRE). (2023). *Annual report 2022-23.* Details the progress of India's renewable energy initiatives.
4. Central Electricity Authority (CEA). (2022). *Report on optimal energy mix 2030.* Examines India's

energy transition towards renewable sources.

5. Forest Survey of India (FSI). (2023). *India state of forest report (ISFR)*. Comprehensive analysis of India's forest cover and afforestation efforts.

Journal Articles

1. Adve, N. (2007). Implications of climate panel report. *Economic and Political Weekly, 42*(12), 1001-1003.
2. Agrawala, S. (1998). Context and early origins of the Intergovernmental Panel on Climate Change. *Climate Change, 39*, 605-620.
3. Arrhenius, S. (1896). On the influence of carbonic acid in the air upon the temperature of the ground. *Philosophical Magazine and Journal of Science, S5, 41*(251), 237-276.
4. Asselt, H. V. (2007). From unity to diversity: The UNFCCC, the Asia-Pacific Partnership, and the future of international law on climate change. *Carbon & Climate Law Review, 1*, 17-28.
5. Asselt, H. V., Gupta, J., & Biermann, F. (2005). Advancing the climate agenda: Exploiting material and institutional linkages to develop a menu of policy options. *Review of European Community & International Environmental Law, 14*, 255-264.
6. Atapattu, S. (2001). Sustainable development, myth or reality? A survey of sustainable

development under international law and Sri Lankan law. *Georgetown International Environmental Law Review, 13*, 76-98.

7. Banuri, T., & Sagar, A. (1999). In fairness to current generations: Lost voices in the climate debate. *Energy Policy, 27*(9), 509-514.
8. Barratt-Brown, E., & others. (1993). A forum for action on global warming: The UN Framework Convention on Climate Change. *Colorado Journal of International Environmental Law and Policy, 4*, 101-112.
9. Wood, J. C. (1996). Intergenerational equity and climate change. *Georgetown International Environmental Law Review, 8*, 293-312.
10. Yamin, F. (2001). NGOs and international environmental law: A critical evaluation of their roles and responsibilities. *RECIEL, 10*(2), 149-162.
11. Yamin, F. (1998). The Kyoto Protocol: Origins, assessment and future challenges. *RECIEL, 7*(2), 113-127.
12. Yohe, G. (2000). Assessing the role of adaptation in evaluating vulnerability to climate change. *Climatic Change, 46*, 371-390.
13. Kumar, A., & Sahni, S. (2020). Renewable energy in India: Challenges and opportunities. *Energy Policy Research Journal, 45*(2), 121-135.
14. Rao, N. D., & Min, J. (2018). Decent living

standards: Material prerequisites for human wellbeing. *Nature Sustainability, 1*(11), 632-639.

15. Sharma, S. (2019). Climate change and sustainable urban development in India. *International Journal of Environmental Planning, 14*(3), 211-223.
16. Singh, R. K., & Jha, M. (2021). Climate-resilient agriculture in India: Practices and policies. *Agricultural Science & Technology, 36*(4), 421-432.

International Reports

1 Intergovernmental Panel on Climate Change (IPCC). (2023). *Climate change 2023: Impacts, adaptation, and vulnerability*. Highlights India-specific vulnerabilities and adaptation strategies.

2 World Bank. (2022). *India's pathways to decarbonization: A sectoral analysis*. Discusses India's efforts to achieve net-zero emissions.

3 International Energy Agency (IEA). (2021). *India energy outlook 2021*. Provides a global perspective on India's energy transition.

4 United Nations Environment Programme (UNEP). (2022). *The emissions gap report 2022*. Assesses global progress, with insights into India's

contribution.

Online Resources

1. PRS Legislative Research. (2023). *Climate change and India: Policy framework and challenges.* https://prsindia.org
2. Down to Earth. (2023). *India's renewable energy revolution.* https://downtoearth.org.in
3. The Energy and Resources Institute (TERI). (2023). *Climate and energy transition in India.* https://www.teriin.org
4. Climate Action Tracker. (2023). *India's climate targets and actions.* https://climateactiontracker.org

Case Studies and News Articles

1. The Hindu. (2023). *India's progress in achieving its INDC goals.*
2. Economic Times. (2023). *India's green bonds: A step*

towards climate finance.

3. Mongabay India. (2023). *Mangrove conservation in India's coastal regions.*
4. BBC News. (2023). *India's role at COP28: A climate leadership perspective.*
5. Business Standard. (2023). *Electric mobility in India: Opportunities and challenges.*

ABOUT THE AUTHOR

Gaurav Kumar Shandilya

Gaurav Kumar Shandilya is a dedicated scholar and researcher with a rich academic background and diverse interests. Holding master's degrees in Anthropology and Physics, he has qualified the National Eligibility Test (NET) and is currently pursuing his research as a scholar. A graduate of the prestigious Ramjas College, University of Delhi, his work reflects a deep understanding of interdisciplinary studies.

Apart from academic pursuits, Gaurav is also an accomplished writer. He has published an e-book of self-written Hindi poetry, showcasing his passion for literature, and has contributed numerous research articles to esteemed journals. Residing in Dhanbad, Jharkhand, he draws inspiration from the natural world and societal dynamics, which is evident in his writings.

In Rain, Temperature, and Climate Change in India, Gaurav combines his expertise and dedication to explore the critical intersection of climate change and human rights in India, making this book a valuable contribution to the field.

BOOKS BY THIS AUTHOR

कविता कीबोर्ड

This is a hindi poetry collection with ISBN NO : 978-93-341-2553-5

Research Papers

The author has published several research papers in prestigious journals.

AFTERWORD

As I conclude Rain, Temperature, and Climate Change in India, I reflect on the immense journey this book represents not just for me as an author, but for the collective efforts to address one of the most urgent challenges of our time. Climate change is no longer a distant threat; its effects are visible in every corner of our country, affecting the lives and rights of millions.

Through this work, I sought to explore the profound connections between climate change, human rights, and the efforts made to combat this crisis. The journey of researching, writing, and analyzing has been as humbling as it has been enlightening. I hope this book not only informs readers about the gravity of the situation but also inspires them to take action in their own capacities. From policymakers to grassroots advocates, the responsibility to protect our environment and ensure justice for all is a shared one.

I express my heartfelt gratitude to everyone who has engaged with this book. Your interest signifies the first step toward understanding and contributing to the solution. Let us move forward together in preserving the balance of nature, safeguarding human rights, and creating a sustainable future for generations to come.

Gaurav Kumar Shandilya

ACKNOWLEDGEMENT

I extend my deepest gratitude to all those who supported me in completing this book, Rain, Temperature, and Climate Change in India.

First, I thank my mentors and professors, whose guidance and encouragement have been instrumental in shaping my academic journey. I am also grateful to the researchers and institutions whose work provided the foundation for this study.

To my family and friends, your unwavering belief in me and my work has been a source of strength.

Lastly, I dedicate this book to the tireless efforts of every individual working to conserve nature and combat climate change. Your commitment inspires this endeavor.

Gaurav Kumar Shandilya

www.ingramcontent.com/pod-product-compliance
Lightning Source LLC
LaVergne TN
LVHW050313160826
845677LV00014B/3376
* 9 7 8 9 3 3 4 1 6 1 8 6 1 *